THE TRIALS OF MICHAEL JACKSON

THE TRIALS

OF

MICHAEL

JACKSON

LYNTON GUEST

Aureus

For Tim Wilson
A true friend and inspiration

Also by Lynton Guest
With Alex Fynn and Peter Law:
The Secret Life of Football
With Alex Fynn:
Heroes & Villains
Out of Time
For Love or Money

First published in 2006
Second edition 2009
© 2006 Lynton Guest

ISBN 10: 1-899750-40-1
ISBN 13: 978-1-899750-40-5

Inside front sleeve photographs of CBS building (Black Rock) and Sony Headquarters in New York courtesy of Jeff Hutchison.

A catalogue record for this book is available from the British Library.
Typeset by Andrew Buckley, Clunton, Shropshire.
Printed in Great Britain.

Aureus Publishing Limited
Castle Court
Castle-upon-Alun
St Bride's Major
Vale of Glamorgan
CF32 0TN
Tel: (01656) 880033 Fax (01656) 880033
International Tel/Fax: +44 1656 880033
E-mail: sales@aureus.co.uk
Website: www.aureus.co.uk

CONTENTS

ACKNOWLEDGEMENTS

Many people have given considerable help in the production of this book. I would like to pay a special tribute to Meuryn Hughes for his support, forbearance and tolerance during what at times has been a turbulent period. I would also like to extend my heartfelt thanks to everyone else at Aureus Publishing.

Thanks are due to a number of people who cannot be named, especially those at the Sony Corporation and Sony BMG. Confidentiality is an important element for writers and although it is a shame that those who contributed most to this story must forego public recognition, they know who they are and I want to say thank you to all of them.

In the process of writing this book, I am grateful to have received considerable help from Paul Russell and Les Molloy, not only for the information they provided, but also for some interesting days at Wentworth and even more interesting nights at the Groucho club.

In addition, the following have given me facts, opinions, moral support, general help and some wonderful insights. In no particular order they are: James Guest, Robert Boyd, Alex Fynn, Gerald O'Connell, Mark Rooney, Sirena Guest Bergman, Jimmy Edwards, Walter Yetnikoff, Jeff Hutchison, John McIndoe, George McIndoe, Gary Dyson, Angie Guest, Carly Williams, Sven Gusevik, Russell Haddington, Jane Clinton, Terry Marsh, Tony Cook, Barrie Barlow, George Williams, Matt Thompson-Royds, Barry Rose, Philippa Lawson, Tracey Wilson, Peter Clarke, Andrew Croker, Gloria Boyd, Dominic Turnbull, Kiki King, Steve Gardner, Tim Gunn, John Kaufman, Peter Law, Professor Greg McClatchey, Michelle Clarke, TAN Menon, James Tapper, Nicola Jones, Robert Stigwood, Teresa Sulyok, Julia Richards, Gary Prado, Rolando Aguilera, Ron Usher, Ray Jones, Richard Watson, Matthew Wright, Daniel Wolf, Tim Wilson, Lucas Wilson, and all those at the Japanese Embassy in London.

Finally, I owe extra-special thanks to Julia and Margarite for such tenderness, to Sheena and Merle for making sure I wasn't a gooseberry and to Juliann Baker for the excitement of several lifetimes. Thank you.

Lynton Guest: London, July 2006

INTRODUCTION

This book came about as a result of a chance conversation with someone whose knowledge of, and experience in, the highest echelons of the music industry are second to none. During the course of the exchange I was given some information about Michael Jackson which was unknown to the public. With the singer on trial in California, everyone was gossiping about the case in their spare time, including me.

In the words made famous during the Watergate scandal of the 1970s, I began to 'follow the money'. As an historian, researcher and journalist I knew from the information I received that there was something being hidden or obscured that was much bigger and more important than we were being told at the time. I could just feel it. Little by little, as I ranged from London, via New York and California, all the way to Tokyo, the incredible story contained in these pages began to reveal itself.

During the course of this journey I have also plundered my own past, to try to make sense of some of the things I was discovering. By including this material, I hope to show that the events central to this book are not part of some one-off aberration, but have been woven into the fabric of the music business since its inception. Anyone who loves music or who is a fan of any artist should read on. The dark underbelly of the entertainment world is not a pretty sight. It is time to hold it up to the light.

1

JESSE JACKSON SAID

'Not Guilty.'

Again and again these two little words from the voice of the jury foreman, Paul Rodriguez, reverberated around the courtroom. There was one count of conspiracy to kidnap and falsely imprison an entire family, four counts of committing lewd acts, one count of attempting to commit a lewd act, four counts of supplying alcohol to minors and a number of counts on lesser charges arising from the same crimes, allegedly committed against an underage boy, Gavin Arvizo. These last counts were offered to the jury as alternatives should they find the accused innocent of the main indictments. Instead, they found the defendant not guilty on all charges. From the small community of Santa Maria in Southern California to the furthest corners of the world, astonishment registered. But just as OJ Simpson discovered some years previously, Michael Jackson was about to find out that a not guilty verdict does not an innocent man make in the eyes of commentators and consequently, the public. Had a blatant child molester beat the rap? If not, could the adverse reaction be yet another manifestation of the racial fault lines carving an inexorable swathe through American society? Perhaps it was simply a case of celebrity-bashing for no good reason, unlikely though that might seem to most of us. Or had something been going on that was more sinister than any of these?

These questions had perplexed me since about two-thirds of the way through Michael Jackson's infamous trial. One spring afternoon in 2005 I happened to be at the home of Paul Russell, delightfully situated among the lush trees surrounding the famous Wentworth golf course in Surrey, about forty minutes drive from London. Paul Russell knows Michael Jackson. As a senior Vice-President of Sony Music Entertainment and before that as an executive with CBS Records, Russell worked with the singer regularly. Their association goes back to the 1970s, when the Jackson 5 quit Motown to sign with CBS. Moreover, Russell spent time socialising with Jackson during those years. Paul Russell and I, along with the doyen of British record promotion men, Les Molloy, were sitting in the office complex which is attached to Russell's house, discussing the production of the now-retired record executive's autobiography. As we shared a glass or two of wine, Paul lit a huge cigar and began giving his views on the progress of Michael Jackson's trial.

'There's one thing I just don't get,' Paul ventured.

'What's that?'

'Well,' said Paul, 'it's this business of the drink, the alcohol. You can say what you like about the rest of it, but the drink charges make no sense to me, no sense at all.'

'How do you mean?'

'Look, I've been around Michael for years, decades. I've been with him at formal and informal occasions. I've been at private dinners with him when only four or five other people were present. I've flown across the Atlantic with him and Lisa-Marie (Presley). In all those years I have never, ever seen him take one drop of alcohol.'

Paul shrugged his shoulders and took another puff on his Davidoff.

The import of what Russell said was astounding. Apart from the molestation and conspiracy charges, Michael Jackson had been accused of plying his accusers – the youngsters of the Arvizo family – with alcohol to get them drunk and have his wicked way. In support of this contention the prosecution produced witnesses, most notably a number of flight attendants from the private airline Jackson used for his travels, who said that the King of Pop concealed his own drinking by asking them to pour away the cola from soft drink cans and replace it with vodka or white wine, which he then drank copiously during the flights. Jackson's alleged drinking was not central to the truth or otherwise of the molestation charges but, in common with many US prosecutors, the Santa Barbara District Attorney, Tom 'Mad Dog' Sneddon, and his assistants, Ron Zonen, and Gordon Auchinloss, who were in charge of the prosecution case, seemed addicted to overkill. But so marginal was Jackson's own alleged drinking to the case that it begged the question; why would the issue of Jackson's drinking be introduced at all if there were any doubt about it?

Giving alcohol to minors was put forward as corroborating evidence to the main charges, which were concerned with the committing of lewd acts. Whether Jackson himself drank or not was surely irrelevant to these accusations. Yet Paul Russell is no fool. Record company executives develop, out of necessity, a perceptive eye for their artists' drug and drink usage. Russell even knew why Michael Jackson maintained a large wine cellar. 'When Michael bought Neverland,' Paul said, 'someone told him that no house was complete without a wine cellar, so he arranged to have one put in, and being Michael, he had to have the best, but he never drank any of the wine himself, at least not to my knowledge.'

Put it this way: I completely trusted Paul Russell's veracity and his judgment on this one. He certainly had no reason to lie (indeed in the course of our discussions over his autobiography he told me of any number of incidents featuring himself and his associates which were far worse than Jackson's supposed alcohol use) and he was expert at knowing what his artists were up to. You should hear his stories of getting blind drunk again and again with the manager and producer of Abba, the Swede, Stig Anderson, as they conducted their contractual negotiations each November. It seemed to me there was no way Michael Jackson could have been a secret drinker without Russell being aware of the fact. So what was going on? Something didn't smell right.

That night Paul Russell checked his recollections with a colleague in the USA in case his memory was failing him. The word came back that he had remembered correctly. His opinion about Jackson's drinking was confirmed. But that confirmation went against the prevailing wisdom. Just about everyone I spoke to believed, if not the main allegations, certainly that Jackson was a secret drinker. At my instigation, Russell repeated his knowledge of this issue to some members of the great British press a few days later. Yet despite their avarice at the time for Jackson stories, they were all expecting a guilty verdict, on the alcohol charges if nothing else. Indeed I would go so far as to say that most of them (for professional reasons of course), wanted a guilty verdict. This prejudiced them against the exclusive story staring them in the face and for whatever reason, they refused to believe it. Thus a major Michael Jackson scoop, which would later be verified by the jury's verdict, lost out to the media's already-decided agenda.

Chapter 1

It was entirely different a month or so earlier, when Paul gave me information concerning Michael Jackson's finances. There had been speculation throughout the run-up to the trial that the defendant was in financial trouble. The prosecution sought to introduce the state of Jackson's money problems at every turn before the trial and during the proceedings. They claimed that Michael Jackson was, to all intents and purposes, bankrupt. The reason they gave for their concentration on this point was that if it were true, it provided a motive for Jackson to have given the broadcaster, Martin Bashir, virtually unlimited access to his life. The prosecution line was that Jackson needed money following a downturn in his record sales in the 1990s. Bashir, through the proposed television documentary, *Living with Michael Jackson*, offered the prospect of bringing the fading star back into the public eye, thereby helping Jackson generate vast amounts of cash once again. This, they said, was the pivotal event which precipitated the abuse of Gavin Arvizo.

The lawyers in the Santa Barbara DA's office obviously do not know very much about the way the entertainment industry works. The fact is, artists live for the publicity they generate. It's what they believe makes them whole. Whether or not Jackson's finances were on the skids, he would probably still have wanted to do the show with Bashir. Although the prosecution, at great expense, employed a forensic accountant to verify their claims, the exact nature of Jackson's finances remained a matter of dispute.

The story Paul Russell told me then was even more extraordinary than the one concerning Jackson's supposed alcohol consumption. It turned out that Michael Jackson was indeed in something of a financial hole, although he was far from bankrupt. The details, as they rolled out of Russell's mouth, were jaw-dropping. His knowledge came from the fact that he was, in addition to holding responsibilities at the record label, also Chairman of a music publishing company called Sony ATV, which was a joint venture between Sony and Michael Jackson. Jackson was a director and major stockholder in the company, owning fifty per cent of the shares.

Sony ATV was originally formed under the name Associated Television (ATV) in the UK during the 1950s. It was founded by one of Britain's greatest impresarios, Lew Grade. Grade was of one of a family of long-established show-business agents and entrepreneurs that included Bernard Delfont, Leslie Grade and, later, Michael Grade, who at the time of writing is Chairman of the BBC. Back in the fifties, Lew Grade also started the Independent Television Corporation (ITC), which provided programmes such as *The Prisoner*, starring Patrick McGoohan, *The Saint*, with Roger Moore and *The Persuaders*, which featured Moore and Tony Curtis, to British and international broadcasters. ATV was itself originally one of these broadcasters, having been awarded a franchise in the mid 1950s to operate one of the new commercial television companies in the UK. ATV broadcast to the English Midlands as part of the Independent Television Network (ITV).

Grade was also involved with another old-school show business tycoon, Louis Benjamin, in one of the three major record companies existing in Britain at the time. This company was called Pye Records, which, along with EMI and Decca, accounted for the vast majority of records sold in the country. ATV acquired Pye as a wholly-owned subsidiary in 1957 with Lew Grade and Louis Benjamin holding most of the shares. Another subsidiary company, ATV Music Publishing, was created to exploit a catalogue of songs, mainly written by or for artists on the Pye label or for themes to ITC and ATV television programmes. It also bought the UK rights to some classic rock and roll music coming out of the USA.

When a song is commercially recorded it is the job of the song's publisher to register it with the appropriate agencies, such as the Performing Rights Society. If the song proves to be a money-earner, the publisher collects royalties from sales and fees which are payable each time the tune is played on radio, television, film or other reproductive medium, like ringtones. The publisher then pays a previously agreed portion of the money collected to the writer(s) of the song.

If this sounds like a model of efficiency, it isn't. Like any industry, the music business contains its fair share of vendettas, petty rivalries and office politics. Unlike other industries, though, there is so much money sloshing around, much of it unaccounted for (many would say it is also undeserved), that egos can reach stratospheric levels and responses are often wildly disproportionate. In my experience, the 'prima donna' factor goes up in inverse proportion to the level of talent.

Back in the late 1970s and early 1980s, for instance, when I was running with Angie Guest a small, independent record label, we went out to a working breakfast with an old-time music publisher with whom I was negotiating over the payment of monies for the promotion of a record.

Chapter 1

Publishers make huge profits from songs which are commercially successful but they are often loath to spend any of this profit on promotion, preferring to leave it to the record company, the management or sometimes, the artists themselves. Publishers can rationalise this because if one particular version of a song doesn't sell well, there could always be another cover of it next year or in five years time. For the publisher, if only one of these is viable, the company makes money. Publishers, to be fair, cannot spend cash every time someone records one of the songs under their control but it is part of the necessary skill of a publisher to be able to differentiate between those covers which have a chance of success and those that don't.

The song that concerned us at the breakfast was – and is still – known throughout the world. It was 'My Way', and its success was in no small measure due to the words, written by Paul Anka. The publisher, who had already downed a half bottle of the finest Scotch whisky by the time I arrived, was in full flow. In fact, on that day he was extremely irritated. The reason for this was a version of 'My Way', recorded by Sid Vicious of the Sex Pistols. In those days, punk was new and challenging the status quo that existed in the music business at the time. Many old-school movers and shakers felt threatened by the punk movement and set their faces against it in all its forms. However, once a song has been recorded and made available to the masses (i.e. once it is in the public domain), anyone can make a version of it and release it without having to ask permission. As long as any publishing royalties that accrue from sales or airplay are paid and the writer and publisher receive their due credit, there are few restrictions. Anyone would think this would promote a genteel atmosphere but at our breakfast the publisher of 'My Way' was apoplectic. He hated the Sid Vicious treatment of the song and would have stopped its release if he could but there was nothing he could do.

However, when it comes to the use of a song in a movie or television programme, it is a different story. In these cases, permission from the publisher to use the song for such a purpose is required. The technical term for this is the synchronisation rights. The Sex Pistols had made a film called *The Great Rock & Roll Swindle*, the climax of which featured Sid Vicious singing 'My Way' on stage before shooting the audience, which was made up of the great and the good, with a machine gun. This was too much for the publisher. As he drank more whisky, he became ever-more vehement that he would not grant permission for 'My Way' to be used in the movie.

He had already held up the release of the film for some months by the time of our breakfast. I argued with him for about an hour, telling him that pop music was supposed to be about outrage, not safe, family-oriented fare. I reminded him of how Elvis shocked America with his pelvic gyrations during the fifties and how every parent hated the Rolling Stones in the sixties but he would not be moved. He even justified his position by claiming that Paul Anka himself would agree with his decision. My secondary argument, that it was not the job of a music publisher to be the arbiter of public taste, similarly cut no ice.

It took many more months before he finally relented and allowed 'My Way' to be included in *The Great Rock & Roll Swindle*. As is usually the case, what eventually changed his mind was money. The Sex Pistols became too big to turn down, the movie would generate a large income, and the prospect of losing these revenues overcame his abhorrence of the Sid Vicious version. After a considerable amount of cash changed hands, the necessary permission was granted.

As for Lew Grade, rather than base the publishing arm of ATV in Birmingham, where his television operation was located, he established it at the headquarters of Pye Records, situated just off Edgware Road, near Marble Arch in central London.

Times were good for both the Grade family and their companies in the 1950s and 60s. The television operation, which held a monopoly of advertising revenues in the region to which it broadcast, was part of the system that was famously labelled 'a licence to print money', by another ITV mogul, Lord Thomson. As such it could hardly fail to be anything other than wildly profitable. Meanwhile, Pye Records was at the forefront of the British music explosion of the 1960s. EMI might have given us the Beatles and Decca the Rolling Stones, but Pye churned out its fair share of hits during the decade up to 1970. The company released music by, among others, The Searchers, the Kinks, Donovan, the Moody Blues and Mungo Jerry. The label's most popular artist was, for years, the internationally successful Petula Clark, whose most famous hit was 'Downtown'. Just like ATV with its publishing, Pye also had contracts with a number of US labels to manufacture their records and distribute their music in the UK. Among these was Chess Records, one of America's seminal R&B (Rythm and Blues) record companies, which numbered Chuck Berry among its roster of artists.

Chapter 1

In 1968, the now-knighted Sir Lew Grade pulled off what turned out to be one of his greatest coups, although it wasn't seen as such at the time. In terms of earning power into the future, nothing could come close to his acquisition for ATV Music of the rights to the Lennon and McCartney catalogue, featuring every song written by the pair up to the Beatles' final split in 1971. The Beatles' manager, Brian Epstein, had started a company called Northern Songs in the early sixties as a vehicle for Lennon and McCartney's song publishing. This company was administered and part-owned by an old-style publisher in London's Denmark Street (known as Tin Pan Alley), named Dick James. James was originally a crooner best known for singing the theme music to a famous children's television show, Robin Hood, which was financed by Lew Grade's company, ITC. James soon gave up singing, however, and became a music publisher with his own company, Dick James Music. Northern Songs was administered by Dick James through this company, which meant that it was James who collected royalties every time a Beatles' record was sold or played on the radio. This type of arrangement has become common in the intervening years, although the royalty percentage paid to the actual writers these days is far higher than Dick James would ever have countenanced back in the 1960s. The split then was fifty per cent to Northern Songs (essentially Dick James) and fifty per cent to Lennon and McCartney. Out of their share, the two songwriters also had to pay management commission to Brian Epstein.

When Epstein died in 1967, the Beatles' empire was thrown into disarray and confusion. Dick James, who was coming up to his retirement, subsequently put Northern Songs up for sale and John Lennon and Paul McCartney attempted to buy it, wanting, quite reasonably, to gain ownership of the publishing rights to their songs. Obviously, Lennon and McCartney were extremely upset that the songs they wrote were not theirs to do with as they wished. When the Beatles first arrived on the scene they were happy to sign any deal put in front of them by Epstein. As naïve youngsters (like Epstein in many ways), this is not surprising. It was only when the unimagined success of the Beatles transformed the music industry (and the world) that writers and performers began to receive a higher percentage of earnings. However, Lennon and McCartney's bid, which was part of a long and acrimonious battle for Northern Songs, failed, and the superior financial muscle of Sir Lew Grade, the two Beatles' adversary in the bidding war, ensured that their music passed into the control of ATV.

ATV Music Publishing went from strength to strength during the 1970s. Under its head, Len Beadle, it signed up many songwriters and bought numerous catalogues, including the raft of music written by song-writing geniuses, Lieber and Stoller. This catalogue contained songs recorded by Elvis Presley, such as Hound Dog and Jailhouse Rock, as well as most of Little Richard's greatest hits. Along with the continuing royalties accruing from Lennon and McCartney's music, these new deals ensured that ever more amounts of cash rolled in. ATV Music was fast becoming the jewel in Sir Lew Grade's crown.

Although the television arm of the Grade organisation performed well for a while, ATV eventually lost its government-granted television licence and the midlands franchise was awarded to a revamped company, Central Television, in which Grade held a minority interest. Moreover, ITC lost a packet on an ill-conceived film venture called *Raise the Titanic* and the fortunes of Pye began to wane as the 1970s drew to a close. Pye still produced hits through the seventies, most notably with songs like 'Kung Fu Fighting' by Carl Douglas and the label had major success with material licensed from the USA, such as all of the great Barry White's recordings, but there was no doubt that Pye's heyday was over.

The reasons for Pye's demise are an object lesson in the music business. An example of what occurred can be seen in the story of one of the members of the band, Mungo Jerry. Mungo Jerry are best remembered for their world-wide hit, 'In The Summertime', which was released on one of Pye's offshoot labels, Dawn Records. The band's producer, Barry Murray, found the song while on holiday in France. When he arrived back in London from his vacation, Murray procured English lyrics and an international hit was born. The guys of Mungo Jerry actually started out as lovers of folk-blues of the Leadbelly variety. Their guitarist, Paul King, being something of a purist, soon left the band for a solo career, wanting to remain closer to his roots as a country bluesman than did the rest of the band, who had embarked on a more commercial phase of their development. As well as his solo work, Paul achieved cult status with the King-Earl Boogie Band. Now Pye had been somewhat left behind at the start of the 1970s by the shift in popularity from singles to albums and those in charge of the label were still wedded to the concept that artists' careers were reliant on the success of 45s. Unfortunately for Pye, its contract with Paul King, signed when Mungo Jerry were at their peak, called for the label to commit itself to financing, recording and promoting a solo album by Paul. The truth was, though, the record company's heart wasn't really in it.

One day, Paul played some of his new songs to me and my associate, Jimmy Edwards, at the house we shared at Sunbury-on-Thames, just outside London. Edwards had made his name as a leading member of the art-pop band 'Neat Change' who had been gathering momentum through playing some blistering gigs on the London club scene in the sixties. The tracks Paul King played us were good, heartfelt songs of some originality and deserved to be promoted as much as anything by Crosby, Stills and Nash or other stars of the time. On the surface, they were not as commercial as the sing-along chirpiness of Mungo Jerry but in those days what was commercial was being re-defined almost daily. As things turned out, Pye spent a fair amount of money on Paul King, but it was in a grudging manner, unlikely to produce positive results. Paul's songs, including some produced by Jimmy Edwards and myself under a contract negotiated on our behalf by the greatest of all music industry businessmen, Robert Stigwood, did not receive the promotional effort they undoubtedly deserved. There were some who claimed that Pye deliberately failed to promote the album, entitled 'Been in the Penn too Long', because the company wanted rid of Paul King, Thus Pye lost money on a venture that, due to the success of Mungo Jerry, should have been a stick-on winner. Their actions did, however, force a bitter Paul King out of Pye. Ironically, by the millennium, many of the Dawn label's productions, including Paul King's but not Mungo Jerry's, had become collectors' items.

So Pye, and to some extent, ATV and ITC, were being left behind by changes in the way the music and television businesses worked. In 1977, Sir Lew Grade was elevated to the status of peer of the realm. He took the title, Lord Grade. But the upheavals in his commercial domain meant the companies he controlled would have to adapt or die. His peerage would be of no help unless such a transformation took place. Perhaps Lord Grade had passed his own sell-by date by then because by the mid-1980s both Pye Records and ATV Music were up for sale. The music publishing company was bought by the Australian businessman, Robert Holmes Acourt (sometimes spelt in the Old French 'à Court'). Acourt was a quintessential eighties entrepreneur who disposed of the assets he acquired from Grade in double quick time and at great profit to himself. In the same deals, hundreds of people were thrown out of their jobs. This was particularly true of the workers in the old Pye (renamed PRT) building near Marble Arch in London. The Pye Records catalogue was soon disposed of, while ATV's music publishing arm was, after yet another fierce bidding war, sold to Michael Jackson, who used $47 million dollars of his royalties from 'Thriller' to fund the purchase.

Many people have sought to take the credit for 'persuading' Michael Jackson to buy ATV Music. In fact, he needed no persuading and although the deal with Holmes Acourt was hammered out by Jackson's lawyer, John Branca, it was Jackson himself who was always the prime mover.

The news that Michael Jackson had bought the Beatles catalogue caused a sensation. What was not known was that there was one famous Lennon and McCartney song that wasn't included in the deal. Robert Holmes Acourt had a daughter called Penny and Acourt signed over the rights to 'Penny Lane' to her as a present. ATV has tried many times over the years to buy back the song to complete the set but Penny has always resisted the temptation to sell. Considering that this one song alone produces over a million dollars a year in royalty income, it is not surprising that she prefers to hang on to it.

Extrapolating from this number for a moment, my estimate is that each year, at 2006 prices, the Lennon and McCartney songs in the Sony ATV catalogue pull in some $200 million of royalty income, split between the publisher and the writers (in the case of John Lennon, his estate).

After Michael Jackson's deal with Robert Holmes Acourt for ATV Music, it was reported that Paul McCartney was furious with Jackson because Jackson's acquisition meant that Macca lost the chance to regain control of his old songs. It is a charge that has been repeated and expanded upon down the years. All kinds of conversations, arguments and assertions have perpetuated the myth. My information is that this is not an accurate reflection of the facts. Michael Jackson believed he should find out whether McCartney or John Lennon's widow, Yoko, had any objections to him buying the catalogue. If Jackson thought either of them was against his purchase he would have pulled out of the deal but word came back that they were not. They had spurned a previous opportunity to buy ATV Music themselves in 1981. This is not so surprising when you think about it. Undoubtedly, both Paul and Yoko could have raised the necessary cash but still, $47 million is a considerable amount of money. Moreover, if either of them had acquired the songs, the other would probably not have been too pleased. And it is inconceivable that Paul and Yoko could have worked together. Michael Jackson had oodles of cash after 'Thriller' and he certainly possessed artistic credibility. That would have made him an acceptable party to both Paul and Yoko. Paul McCartney has been quoted many times concerning Jackson's purchase of ATV. Some of the things he is reported to have said have been extremely negative while others have bordered on acceptance. It is difficult to discern exactly what McCartney thought at the time or thinks now. One of McCartney's main beefs was not Jackson's ownership *per se* but the fact that the royalty rate paid to himself and John Lennon's estate was determined when the two Beatles were youngsters and was far too low. That is not an unreasonable position in my view. In contrast, Yoko Ono Lennon has remained constant in her support for Jackson's acquisition, at one time calling it 'a blessing'.

One of the great complaints of Lennon and McCartney when Sir Lew Grade bought their music was that their songs were now owned by 'men in suits'. Michael Jackson was certainly not of that ilk. Indeed, Jackson professed his love of the music he had bought and saw himself as someone who could look after the legacy the songs embodied. As Paul Russell put it, 'I remember in the early days, just after he (Jackson) bought the Beatles catalogue, he was so enthusiastic and earnest about owning what he saw as part of music history. He wanted to be a guardian of the Beatles' memory, not make a fortune out of them.'

Sadly, it did not stay that way. At around the same time that Jackson bought ATV Music, his record label, CBS, which, like ATV, had started out as a broadcaster, began negotiations to sell its record division. It was finally bought by the Japanese electronics corporation, Sony, in 1988, for $2 billion. After a frantic series of meetings and arguments over the price, the deal was finally sealed during a concert in Tokyo by none other than Michael Jackson. The sale was completed while Jackson was actually on stage, although I can't say which song he was singing at the time.

After the success of its takeover of CBS Records, Sony, seeking to break out of its core business of hardware manufacturing into the software world of music, films and games, looked for further opportunities. One of the imperatives was to expand the company's music publishing interests. Accordingly, the Japanese corporation made Michael Jackson an offer he couldn't refuse. Sony bought 50% of Jackson's shares in ATV Music for $50 million. This was a great piece of business for Michael Jackson, who essentially ended up owning half of the Beatles' publishing rights for nothing. The new company, which owned some of the greatest songs of all time, was renamed Sony ATV. Sony provided the administrative expertise and installed Paul Russell as Chairman of the new entity. Michael Jackson was a director and attended board meetings religiously. There was, however, a huge flaw at the heart of the company. With each party owning fifty per cent, both had to agree before anything could be done. No one wielded enough clout to impose decisions. Even worse, both held the power of veto. If either one didn't consent to something, it wasn't going to happen.

It was from his vantage point as a former Chairman of Sony ATV that Paul Russell was able to reveal the amazing story of the Jackson finances. 'Thriller', the biggest selling album of all time, sold over fifty million copies, netting Jackson around $100 million in recording performance royalties alone. When other revenue streams are taken into account, the golden egg of 'Thriller' brought Michael Jackson in excess of $200 million. Add to that the marketability of the star in the wake of 'Thriller's' success – he could clear over $1 million dollars net profit per live concert – and you can see the immense wealth the album generated. Now this huge amount would probably last most of us forever but in Michael Jackson's case, it brought with it certain self-inflicted pressures. First, Jackson created a huge organisation with a large number of employees, which he saw as commensurate with his new grand status. It must be remembered that before 'Off the Wall', the careers of the Jackson 5 and thus Michael Jackson were perceived as having passed their peak. Jackson's remarkable success thereafter surprised those supposed to be in the know. For Jackson, shopping and spending became symbols of what he believed to be his inalienable right of being top of the pile. This spending, along with the Neverland venture, drained large amounts of cash from Jackson's fortune. Neverland was not simply a large estate. It was part of a mammoth project which could be called the public relations version of Michael Jackson's existence. With its theme park and zoo, Neverland's ongoing running costs of around $5 million a year would be felt by even the richest of men.

The second major pressure came from Jackson's own expectations of himself. In short, Michael Jackson believed that his subsequent recordings would outsell even the huge numbers 'Thriller' managed. So when 'Bad' sold twenty-five million, a figure most artists would die for, it came as a shock to the singer. Unable to alter his spending habits, Jackson carried on as if everything he recorded was selling as many as 'Thriller'. This might not have had such a catastrophic effect had Jackson not become embroiled in the child abuse allegations made by Jordan Chandler in the mid-nineties. The fallout from the Chandler case eventually depressed Jackson's record sales to those of ordinary, common-or-garden superstars. With Jackson failing to curb his outgoings, something had to give.

Thus on two separate occasions, starting in 1999, Michael Jackson was forced to borrow huge amounts of money, secured against the value of his remaining shares in Sony ATV. The first transaction was in the form of a $100 million loan from the Bank of America. Two years later, the same bank lent Jackson another $70 million. His whole stake in Sony ATV was now mortgaged to the hilt. As Chairman of the publishing company, the paperwork went to Paul Russell. What Russell didn't know was that the parent company, Sony Corporation, not only sanctioned the loan, but manipulated the whole process, as will be outlined later. By 2005, Jackson needed another injection of cash but this time it was decided that the total value of Sony ATV, which was then determined to be around $350 million, wouldn't cover a further loan. Instead, it was suggested that Jackson's interest in another company, Mijack, which published songs written by Jackson himself, be put up as security. When Jackson agreed, the Bank of America came up with another $50 million. Thus Jackson's loans from the Bank of America totalled $220 million. To maintain payment of the interest charges alone, a 'Thriller' a year plus a tour would be necessary. As it was, Jackson's future financial security was hanging by a thread.

I persuaded Paul Russell to take this story to the press. We met one evening at the Groucho club in London's Soho district and were joined by two journalists, the respected and experienced financial reporter, Dominic Turnbull, and showbiz correspondent, Kiki King, who possesses a rare combination of talent and beauty in equal measure and went on to become one of the Daily Mirror's 3 a.m. girls. Over the course of an extremely pleasant evening we gave the two journalists the facts. The resultant article was published on March 20th 2005 in the *Mail on Sunday* under the headline 'Debt-ridden Jacko raises £30m ... by mortgaging all his songs'. This was the first time that details of Michael Jackson's true financial situation had appeared in the public domain. I am not talking here about tales of mega-spending or estimates of earnings, all of which are the subject of continual public speculation. Now, a light was being shone on matters of real substance. I didn't know it then but that article was the beginning of a series of events which would lead to an incredible story of deceit, greed and the lust for power. Furthermore, it would eventually reveal a sordid picture of how the music business, global corporations and the law really operate when the stakes are high enough.

The consequences of the article did not take long to manifest themselves. The day after the *Mail on Sunday*'s exclusive was published other media organisations around the world picked up on the story. The biggest selling British daily, the *Sun*, lifted the *Mail* article wholesale. On March 27th, Michael Jackson gave an extensive interview to Revd Jesse Jackson for the reverend's internet radio show, where the two Jacksons commented on the matter, if somewhat obliquely. Michael Jackson did not deny the story. Instead he said: 'This is tabloid sensationalism kind of gossip'. To that Jesse Jackson replied: 'Some people called and they thought it was about the Sony catalogue'. Jesse Jackson pressed the issue: 'It was suggested by a number of your friends this fight was really about this catalogue issue'. It was the first time anyone had come so close to the truth. Michael Jackson's response was enigmatic. Maybe he didn't want to get into the real facts of his finances. Or perhaps he was under strict orders not to make substantial statements while his trial was going on. Whatever the case, the moment was lost. 'Well, you know,' he said, 'I don't want to comment, I don't want to make a comment – it's a delicate issue. I'll let you make the comment on that one.'

Soon afterwards a strange thing happened. Paul Russell, despite being retired from Sony for two years, received a letter from the corporation's legal division warning him not to reveal any more of what he knew. The letter, which relied on a dubious and arguable legal point to make its case, contained a barely disguised threat of sanctions should Russell say anything further on the matter. 'If Sony's letter had any force,' Paul said, 'it would mean I couldn't say anything about what happened in the music business to anyone for ever.' Sony, which had for years allowed a variety of its executives to write books, appear on television and comment publicly on Michael Jackson's affairs, seemed to be afraid of what might now be revealed by Paul Russell. What on earth was it they were trying to hide?

'You know what?' Russell concluded when we next talked about the subject, 'I don't think he (Jackson) did it (the crime(s) for which he was being tried).' Compare that to the opinion of Jackson on the part of a friend of mine, Tim Wilson, who is as well grounded as anyone I know. 'He's a nonce (British slang for sexual pervert)', Tim announced trenchantly.

It would be fair to say that Tim's viewpoint was more representative of the public's than Paul's. But what is the truth? I had been drawn in and now I wanted to find out. That was the start of a remarkable journey, which went from being a simple search for the probability of Jackson's guilt or innocence on the paedophile charges into a murky world of corporate skulduggery stretching halfway around the globe. It would prove to be a story of double-dealing and the subversion of justice, shocking in its all-embracing breadth.

2

SMOKE AND MIRRORS

As I climbed the creaking steps I was almost overcome by a potent mixture of excitement and foreboding. I needed to pull myself together so I attempted to concentrate on my surroundings. The somewhat dilapidated state of the staircase belied the fact that this building was steeped in a history that stretched back through centuries of Britain's national life. As we reached the top, Max Clifford opened the oak door in front of us and ushered me inside. Clifford spoke to the heavy-set man sitting with his back to the door. The man turned, exhibited a beaming smile, and shook my hand. I took it, trying to remain mindful that I could now be staring into the face of a killer.

I can't say for certain exactly why the case of Michael Jackson so caught my imagination that I wanted to delve further. I admire his talent and respect his talent and application but no more so than many artists. Perhaps I had an agenda of my own. I've always been keen on justice issues but that doesn't explain my interest entirely. Perhaps I was still annoyed by the fallout from the OJ Simpson trial, an event that touched me personally.

In the mid 1970s I spent some time in the USA, mainly in South Florida in a town called Margate, near Fort Lauderdale. As a sports nut I was intrigued by American football, of which we saw virtually nothing in Britain in those days. I asked my next door neighbour, a young guy like myself, to explain the gridiron game to me. At the time, OJ Simpson was in his pomp as the star running back of the Buffalo Bills in particular and the NFL generally. So my neighbour, Chuck, used the televised match-ups in which Simpson played to show me how the game worked. I suppose I kind of developed an affinity with American football through its greatest exponent of the era, OJ Simpson.

By the 1990s and long back in London, I got myself hooked up to the early satellite television services. Within a couple of years, the Simpson scandal broke and for the first time in Britain we were going to see a real trial screened on Sky News, live. British trials are never televisied. We had to wait for the US service, Court TV, to be imported before we were allowed to see anything of criminal proceedings. I watched just about every minute of the coverage as well as all the commentary on American television shows hosted by the likes of Larry King and Geraldo Rivera, so I was pretty much up to speed with the issues involved. When Simpson was found not guilty of murdering his wife and her friend I wasn't surprised. The prosecution, in my view, had played its hand poorly, despite initially appearing to hold good cards. What did surprise me was the reaction, especially in the USA, from the public and the media. It appeared that white Americans were convinced Simpson was guilty, whereas African-Americans believed in his innocence. The media were as one: Simpson did it and had gotten away with murder.

After losing a civil case (where the standard of proof is lower than in a criminal prosecution) for wrongful death brought by the estates of the victims, Simpson found himself *persona non grata* in the USA. Any proposed media appearances or attempts to rehabilitate his career were impossible. Those who had decided Simpson was a murderer were annoyed, to say the least. If they couldn't get him found guilty in the criminal courts, they would sure as hell make sure he could never work in the land of the free again. Somehow, this didn't seem right to me. It was un-American.

Suddenly, it was announced from Los Angeles that OJ Simpson was to visit the UK for an appearance on *Richard and Judy*, a chat show screened in the afternoon on British television. It appeared that the acquitted star was only allowed to put his case outside the USA. Simpson's one other engagement in England involved giving a speech and taking questions at the Oxford Union, the august debating chamber for the students of the various colleges that make up Oxford University. It was one of the most prestigious venues in the world. According to reports, no journalists were to be invited to the Oxford debate, nor would television cameras be allowed to film the proceedings. Simpson's trip soon became massive news all over the world. It had been masterminded by Max Clifford, probably the foremost public relations man on the planet.

At the time I was contributing regularly to the pages of one of Britain's major newspapers, the *Sunday Telegraph*, as a sports journalist. In that capacity I brought to the paper a number of exclusive stories, including the first ever article revealing the existence of a plan on the part of the English Football Association (FA) to smash the power of its long-standing rival, the Football League, and assume control over all aspects of the game. It was this plan which ushered in the greatest change ever seen in, first English, then world, football, the formation of the Premier League. The story emerged after I received a summons from the then head of the FA, Graham Kelly, who briefed me exclusively on the plan. My piece was published by the *Telegraph* in the most prominent position possible and not one word was changed by the sub-editors or the brilliant editor of the sports section at the time, David Grice. In my view Grice's tenure in charge of the *Telegraph*'s sports section has never been bettered, despite the much larger budgets and space allocated today.

Grice's immediate successor, for example, a *Telegraph* journalist called Colin Gibson, with whom I had a number of run-ins, later joined the opposition when he became Head of Public Relations at the FA. Gibson was subsequently fired when he carried out a ham-fisted attempt to drop the coach of England's national team, the Swede, Sven Goran Ericsson, in the mire by passing information to the press concerning Ericsson's sexual affair with another FA employee, Faria Alam. Gibson did this because the FA's new Chief Executive, Mark Palios, had also been carrying on an affair with the alluring Alam and Gibson tried to protect his boss by giving up Ericsson to the press, thereby keeping Palios out of the newspapers. It didn't work. The papers printed both stories and added insult to injury by also revealing the fact that Gibson attempted to keep Palios' involvement out of the public eye.

When I heard that OJ Simpson was coming to England a plan of my own started to form in my mind. If I could convince Max Clifford of my *bona fides* I could gain another scoop for the *Telegraph*. I started to badger Clifford, stressing both my sports background and my knowledge of Simpson's trial. I told Clifford that if he provided me with access to his new client, not only would I tell it like I saw it, but also I would not carry the prejudices that characterised most of the press corps. At the same time I contacted the office of the *Telegraph*'s editor – not the sports editor but the editor of the whole paper – Dominic Lawson. Lawson is a member of a very establishment family whose father was a former Chancellor of the Exchequer and whose brother and sister are both high-profile media performers. Mark Lawson is a columnist and broadcaster, while sister

Nigella is British television's resident domestic goddess, having once been a journalist of some originality. Dominic Lawson professed enthusiasm about my proposal to interview Simpson and agreed to publish the piece if I managed to pull it off.

Amazingly, my campaign with Max Clifford paid dividends, and he invited me to attend Simpson's appearance at the Oxford Union. He further promised to introduce me to Simpson afterwards and indicated the interview was on.

I've been involved in the media business in one form or another since I was sixteen years-old but nothing had prepared me for the mayhem on the lawn outside the Oxford Union in the old University City. There was a forest of huge satellite dishes and arc lights that was the size of a small town. Like some post-modern version of the ancient Silk Road caravan, replete with travellers and showmen, the impression created was more Barnum and Bailey than Walter Cronkite. Every news organisation in the world was camped out, along with some of the most famous presenters television has to offer. It was unbelievable. Of course, interest was heightened even further because none of them was supposed to be allowed in.

I have to say that I was impressed by Simpson's speech, which obviously revolved around his arrest and trial. He gave a vigorous defence of his behaviour and continued, as he does to this day, to deny the charge of murder. I was less impressed by some of the questions that followed, which, given that these were students of Oxford University, supposedly the brightest and best, bordered on the banal. 'How do you think you will be judged by God?' was one less than penetrating enquiry. Simpson dealt with that and all other questions effortlessly. It was, the Union President told me, 'The best attended event the Union has ever held'. The level of world-wide media interest, he said, was unprecedented. Afterwards, Max Clifford took me on that slow walk up the grand old stairs and introduced me to OJ Simpson.

Max Clifford has a love-hate relationship with the British public. They hate his supposed cynicism and manipulation, of which he has often been accused, but they love reading about the scandals he reveals. The first thing to be said about him, though, is surely the fact that everyone in the UK knows who he is. He's a household name and a celebrity in his own right. That's not bad, since he is, after all, a public relations man. Moreover, he has been painted as cynical and manipulative by the same media that cannot wait to employ his services. This is due to Clifford's uncanny nose for a story. He has been behind some of the Great British Scandals of recent years, especially those involving politicians and sex. Being a football fan, my favourite is the one that featured the heritage minister in John Major's government, David Mellor. Mellor was having an extra-marital affair with an unknown actress, Antonia di Sancha. Unfortunately for the minister, when the affair became public, Max Clifford took di Sancha on as a client. As Clifford himself later explained, her story, while interesting, needed more spice to attract the large amounts of cash potentially on offer from a mass-circulation newspaper. Accordingly, Clifford invented a piece of detail with which the story became synonymous and which was soon plastered over many a front page. Mellor, di Sancha's account now claimed, had made love to his paramour dressed in the replica kit of the football team he is renowned for supporting – Chelsea.

I found Max Clifford courteous, intelligent and professional. He's also a nice bloke who lets you know what his principles are and sticks to them. He understands the difference between the frivolity of the kind of story cited above and the serious business of life. But despite David Mellor losing his position as a minister of the crown and the undoubted distress caused to his family, the episode did more for Mellor's profile than any number of speeches in the House of Commons. The public's perception of him also benefited as he journeyed from somewhat pompous politician to something approaching national endearment.

As for OJ Simpson, he was cordial and pleasant and answered every question I asked. I didn't see it as my job to try to trip him up and get him to admit anything. Richard and Judy, under pressure from the rest of a rabid media, had attempted to do that and failed miserably. Simpson was simply too clued up. And he had lived the case 24/7 for almost three years. No one knew more about the minutiae than he did. I felt it more important to probe Simpson's current state of mind, his feelings about his situation and the people who were involved in his case. Although most of his comments were uncontroversial, he did make one statement which was intended as a macabre joke but was, in fact, chilling. I asked him how he was regarded by his home community in Brentwood, California after the verdict. 'Everyone is really supportive and friendly,' he stated. 'They like me better than they like the Browns.' (The Browns were the parents of his murdered wife, Nicole.)

Chapter 2

I do not know whether OJ Simpson murdered Nicole Brown Simpson and Ron Goldman, unlike certain media commentators who claim to know absolutely that Simpson did it. I made this plain in the subsequent article I wrote for the *Telegraph*. I then received a shock. Dominic Lawson refused to publish it because he deemed it insufficiently critical of Simpson. It was the first and only time anything like this ever happened to me. Every journalist has to be thick-skinned enough to know that a piece can be spiked or changes ordered. Most of the time, we just have to accept the fact with equanimity. On this occasion, though, the reasons didn't make sense in journalistic terms. Any reporter would have given his right arm for the scoop. I had interviewed OJ Simpson. In the event, Max Clifford being Max Clifford, there were two other writers apart from myself who were allowed access to the Oxford Union debate, one of whom was a reporter from the University magazine. That is typical Clifford, encouraging a young journalist, especially when there is no exclusive to be sold. Both of their pieces, which reflected the conventional wisdom, were published.

Not one other journalist made it into the Union, although hundreds tried, including all of the big US networks with open cheque books. I was never given any credible reason for Lawson's *volte-face*. The only clue I have ever been able to discern for his decision is that the tone of my piece failed to reflect some deeper political position on the part of the newspaper. As it turned out, I was unwilling to make the alterations necessary to get the article into the paper, so my greatest scoop was scuppered by Lawson's agenda and my obstinacy. The fact that Lawson was summarily fired in 2005 by the new owners of the *Telegraph*, the reclusive Barclay brothers, after the shady dealings of the ousted former owner, Conrad Black, were exposed, was of little consolation.

Thus when the Michael Jackson case loomed into view I was in some respects driven by my experience with OJ Simpson. It is easy to be swept along when we are told what it is we should and shouldn't believe by an all-knowing media. The truth is, those in the media actually know very little for certain but since knowledge is power, news organisations and those pundits that work for them tend to dress up opinions as fact. Nowhere have I witnessed this more than in the case of OJ Simpson.

Whatever the case, I was hooked on the Jackson story. I determined to look further, beyond the headlines. But where on earth to start, that was the question. I decided to go back to first principles and examine the court records and the people involved in the trial to see where it took me.

As just about the whole world knows, the catalyst for Michael Jackson's 2005 trial was the television programme, *Living with Michael Jackson*, made by the British journalist, Martin Bashir, and which was broadcast in February 2003. Bashir's career began as a freelance football reporter and in that capacity he contributed to the *Sunday Times* of London. After moving into television as a reporter for the BBC, he quickly established himself as someone who had the knack of persuading people to talk openly on camera. He did enough to come to the attention of BBC bosses and in 1992 he joined the corporation's flagship current affairs programme, *Panorama*.

While he was with *Panorama* in the early 1990s, Bashir investigated the business dealings of the then coach of the England football team, Terry Venables. The subsequent *Panorama* programme on Venables was, in my opinion, a hatchet job containing little in the way of journalistic merit. My view was formed because as a football reporter myself I have met Venables on several occasions and co-wrote, with Alex Fynn, a football expert and former Deputy Chairman of the world's biggest advertising agency, Saatchi and Saatchi, a book featuring Venables, called *Heroes And Vill*ains. Fynn was a giant of the advertising industry, having started with the two Saatchi brothers, Charles and Maurice, back in the sixties. He fondly remembers this period and characterises it, 'Carry on Advertising', after the comedy films of the time. He was there throughout the company's sensational period of growth during the 1980s, when they became the number one advertising agency in the world. Fynn was fired in 1990 when Charles and Maurice withdrew from the management of the company. The new regime appeared to believe loyalty was a liability. However, Fynn was still under contract so although he was no longer wanted in the advertising division, some role had to be found for him. Thus did Alex Fynn reinvent himself as a sports consultant. He was one of the first people in the UK to understand the growing importance of sports to the world of advertising and had been promoting his ideas within the agency for some time. Accordingly, he was employed as a consultant to Saatchi's Sports, Events and Licencing company. In that capacity he advised organisations such as the Football Association and the Football League. In 1993, while remaining a consultant but more at arms length, he oversaw Saatchi's' expansion in the sporting arena, adding the Rugby Football Union and the British Athletics Federation to the company's portfolio of clients. After two more years he finally severed his links with Saatchis and became a fully independent consultant. In his usual, self-deprecating way he would declare that clubs and federations 'ask me for advice then don't take it'.

Once, when I had the onerous task of visiting Rio de Janeiro and New York City, Fynn contacted the heads of the agency in both cities to tell (some might say warn) them I was on my way. It is a measure of the respect in which Fynn was held that in both places I was looked after like royalty. In New York, I was given an office, a secretary and a bank of telephones for the duration of my stay. In Brazil, the head of Saatchi's proffered me a piece of paper with a telephone number on it and said to me in impeccable English: 'Lynton, you are a friend of Alex's. If there is anything you want while you are here, and I mean anything, call this number. And if you get into any bother with anyone, including the police, call this number straight away.'

The book Fynn and I wrote followed the fortunes of two of London's biggest teams – Arsenal and their traditional rivals, Tottenham Hotspur – for a season following the 1990 World Cup in Italy. Fans were flocking back to the game in their millions as the hooligan-fuelled madness of the 1980s, when crowds dropped and interest waned, came to a welcome end. As luck would have it, Arsenal won the League Championship that season and Spurs won the FA Cup (the two big competitions in the English game), so there was plenty of interest in the book. Venables was Tottenham's coach and manager. During that period, he provided us with access to all of his dealings and although there were times when he sailed close to the wind, there was no question of any criminal intent on Venables' part.

In 1992 I was invited to Venables' dining club in London's up-market Kensington district by a Swiss marketing company called TEAM. Over lunch, the Swiss told me of a proposed new competition being planned by UEFA, the governing body of European football, to replace the European Cup with the Champions League. At the time, the public and those in the world of football were unaware of UEFA's manoeuvres. Despite the obvious advantage that might have come his way, Venables never once sought to ingratiate himself into the proceedings. Indeed, he seemed happiest singing 'Fly Me to the Moon', which sounded pretty good to me. On a different occasion another football writer, Peter Law, and myself spoke to Venables about the potential transfer of a goalkeeper to Tottenham (which did not, in the event, take place). During the discussions, Venables did not display even a hint of impropriety. However, Bashir made some of Venables' behaviour appear like the corruption at Enron. For me, it was a shoddy piece of journalism designed to vilify Terry Venables unfairly and, through the use of sensationalism, enhance Bashir's career.

Bashir's greatest coup came when he interviewed Diana, Princess of Wales, for *Panorama*, in which she admitted infidelities during her marriage to the heir to the British crown, Prince Charles, and spilled the beans on her husband's affair with Camilla Parker-Bowles. Thereafter, as you would expect, Bashir's career really took off. He was eventually poached from the BBC by one of the corporation's competitors, Granada TV, in 1999. It was while he was with Granada that he made *Living with Michael Jackson*. A year after that, when the Jackson furore was at its height, Bashir's place in the top division of journalists was confirmed when he was hired by the American network, ABC, to work on the news magazine, *20/20*.

Bashir's rise was spectacular but not without controversy. There were some odd things going on around the Diana interview, for instance. False bank documents, created by a graphic designer, were utilised, it was said, to help secure Diana's agreement to participate in the programme. These documents purported to show that an employee of Earl Spencer, Diana's brother, had been paid £4000 by Rupert Murdoch's News Corporation, publisher of two of Britain's most notorious and scandal-obsessed newspapers, the *Sun* and the *News Of The World*. The scam's purpose was reportedly to fool the Earl into thinking his family's privacy had been compromised in the ongoing war into which Diana and Charles' relationship had degenerated. It was thought Spencer would then be more likely to support the idea of his sister putting her side of the story into the public domain, through an interview with none other than Martin Bashir. In the ensuing internal investigation, the BBC admitted the existence of the false documents but characterised them in what seems to me a rather odd manner. They were made, the BBC officially stated, 'for graphic purposes' in an investigation into the Royal Family and the security services. Whatever really went on, Bashir was cleared by the BBC of any wrongdoing. No independent enquiry ever took place into the affair.

Bashir has also been admonished by such diverse parties as the Broadcasting Complaints Commission and the Bishop of St Albans, for various misdemeanours revolving around the issue of misrepresentation. This is exactly what he was accused of by Michael Jackson and Jackson's defence team. They alleged that Bashir had secured Jackson's cooperation through false-pretences. The truth or otherwise of that allegation remains unresolved. However, the mystery that is Martin Bashir is only deepened by this cryptic comment from one of Bashir's former colleagues on *Panorama*, the producer, Mark Killick. Killick told London journalist, Ian Herbert, that Bashir had 'got some impressive scalps but there was a big falling out and there was a parting of company. I'm saying no more'.

In the world Martin Bashir inhabits, you're only as good as your last exposé. Once he had wrested the damning words of her infidelity from Princess Diana, he needed even more lurid tales from the famous or infamous to follow it up. There could be no question that his aim in snaring Michael Jackson was to get the singer to show us something at least as sensational as the Diana interview. He had already produced an emotional programme with Louise Woodward, the British nanny charged with and convicted of killing the US baby in her care (she was released after the trial by the judge, who, in a highly unusual ruling, substituted his own verdict of not guilty of murder for the jury's guilty conclusion). The problem for Bashir was that both Princess Diana and Louise Woodward wanted to get their controversial comments into the public domain and the mechanism of a television interview was the perfect forum for them to do so. This would not work with Jackson, who had shown on his famous appearance on *Oprah* that he could handle tricky questions without giving away too much. Indeed, Jackson's performance on *Oprah* in the main consisted of his denials of most of the claims of bizarre behaviour through which he had constructed his image over many years. Therefore, another approach was needed in order to get Jackson to tell us something big. And remember, getting people to reveal intimate things was Bashir's forte. That's why, instead of merely interviewing Jackson, as he did with Diana, Bashir decided to follow the singer around for eight months, hence the title of the documentary, *Living with Michael Jackson*. That way, Bashir and his producers reasoned, Jackson was bound to let something slip, sometime. Which of us, if cameras followed our every move for months on end, would not disclose something, probably accidentally, which could be construed by the whole world as monstrous or shaming, whether true or not?

In television, he who controls the editing equipment holds the power. This meant that Bashir was able to draw Jackson in by telling him what a wonderful father he was, saying, 'It almost makes me weep'. This conversation was cut out of the finished programme. Shots of Jackson holding hands with an adolescent boy, Gavin Arvizo, were there for all to see, however, along with pictures of Arvizo resting his head on the star's shoulder. It was this scene which caused such disquiet among the general public as well as the media, coming as it did a decade after the Jordan Chandler affair first raised questions about Jackson's relationships with young boys, and therefore the nature of the singer's sexuality. However, when viewing the programme as a whole the amazing thing was the paucity of anything really deleterious, in a legal sense, to Michael Jackson. Moreover, nothing Jackson said admitted any criminal wrongdoing. Indeed, while acknowledging that he shared his bedroom with children, the star was at pains to point out that no sexual element existed in these events. Jackson said the sleepovers were innocent and helped him experience the childhood he never had. 'What could be more natural?' he asked Bashir. Given that *Living with Michael Jackson* was a production from the man whose reputation was built on getting people to talk, very little of actual substance was revealed. However, if Bashir's eight months were not to be shown up as a complete waste of time, something had to be salvaged from what was, in effect, a non-event. One of the so-called great scenes, for instance, was the revelation of Michael Jackson on a shopping spree (it has since been suggested that most of what Jackson 'bought' that day was later returned).

At a stretch, by putting inferences into the spaces, the pictures could be interpreted differently and so could Jackson's words, which after all admitted he shared his bedroom with other people's children. The public relations experts at Granada were quick to brief the press in advance of the screening to garner publicity for the programme and boost its ratings. Of course, it was the hand-holding and the bedroom-sharing they wanted to publicise. And publicise it they did, big time. Before one single frame of the programme had been seen by the public, the story was out that it virtually proved Jackson was a paedophile. The marketing worked. When *Living with Michael Jackson* was aired in the USA, 27 million people tuned in, while an astonishing 14 million watched the British screening. These numbers were replicated all over the world.

Eighteen months later, not long before the trial, Bashir conducted a televised interview for *20/20* with the former child actor, Corey Feldman. Feldman, who starred in such movies as *Stand By Me* and *The Goonies* had been a friend of Michael Jackson's since Feldman was thirteen years-old. Over a year before his interview with Bashir, around the time when Jackson's home was raided in late 2003, Feldman appeared on the Larry King show. He told the CNN host that he had 'never seen Michael act in any inappropriate way towards a child; never with me'. Bashir's interview did not add anything to this statement. Indeed Feldman again said: 'He never harmed me and he never harmed any children in front of me.' However, this was not enough for Bashir. Now he persuaded Feldman to add the story that on one occasion when he visited Jackson's home when he was 'thirteen or fourteen', Jackson had shown him a book which contained pictures of naked men and women. Feldman went on: 'The book was focused on venereal diseases and the genitalia and he sat down with me and he explained it to me, showed me some pictures and discussed what those meant.'

Once again the publicity hounds went to work and the interview was claimed as a new, damaging revelation. It was nothing of the sort. In fact, the way Feldman told it, it sounded like Jackson was acting quite responsibly. It did, however, reveal the classic Bashir elements. What was in fact exculpatory to Jackson was dressed up with inferences and marketing to make it appear something it was not. But why did Bashir do this on the verge of Jackson's trial, when it could well have a prejudicial effect? Well, since when have news organisations been in the truth business? They are in the entertainment game and, in the USA in particular, have no qualms about any prejudice they might cause. The combination of celebrity, sex and crime was just too much to resist. Moreover, the timing, coming as it did when 250 police officers raided Neverland, guaranteed maximum ratings.

Strangely, having stoked the fires, Bashir was more than a little reticent when it came to telling his story to the court. He had to be served with a subpoena to get him to appear at all. He then showed up in court attended by a battery of ABC lawyers. Since he was not a witness to any actual wrongdoing (and that, in itself, speaks volumes as Bashir 'lived' with Jackson for the best part of a year), the point of Bashir's appearance in the courthouse was twofold. First and most important, he was called to authenticate a video copy of *Living with Michael Jackson*, which was played to the jury as soon as the prosecution's and defence's opening statements had been completed. In the criminal justice system it is not enough simply to play a tape. The person responsible for the recording has to testify that it is an authentic copy of the tape that was made or broadcast and say something about the circumstances under which it was recorded. The context, if you will. The second reason for Bashir's testimony was to say more about Jackson's behaviour during the eight months of filming. This was supposed to lay the foundation for an explanation of Jackson's motives for engaging in the conspiracy to kidnap and falsely imprison the Arvizos, with which he was later charged.

Bashir was the first witness, a ploy designed by the prosecution to get the trial off to a sensational start, one from which they hoped Jackson could not recover. However, Bashir's evidence did not have the desired effect. It was sensational, certainly, but not in the way the prosecution hoped. Bashir began by taking exception to lead prosecutor Tom Sneddon's initial examination. Sneddon, having verified Bashir's identity, asked him about his career as a maker of video documentaries. Bashir was aghast. 'What do you mean by video documentaries?' he asked snootily, 'I call them current affairs films.' Sneddon then asked Bashir which companies he had worked for in his time as a reporter. Having stated that he 'started at the BBC', Bashir looked incredulous when Sneddon followed up by asking, 'What is the BBC?' It was not an auspicious opening. For the rest of Sneddon's questioning, Bashir was variously described as being irritated, perplexed or uncomfortable. The main point for Sneddon, though, was that he got the video of *Living with Michael Jackson* into evidence. Now he could suggest that all manner of nefarious deeds took place in its wake.

After basking in the publicity of his Jackson show, Bashir now courted even more column inches by refusing to answer questions put to him under cross-examination by Jackson's defence attorney, the silvery-maned Tom Mesereau. Mesereau was scathing in his description of Bashir. 'He wanted to do a documentary on Michael Jackson,' Mesereau said. 'He wanted it to be scandalous and he wanted to get rich.'

When a journalist refuses to answer questions in court it is usually because there is an issue about revealing a confidential source. This is a well-trodden path and an honourable course of action since a failure to preserve anonymity after having promised to do so to an informant would result in the press being unable to convince people to give information which might be in the public interest. However, in the case of Martin Bashir, no such issue existed. A refusal to answer while on the witness stand in such circumstances would normally be rewarded by a citation for contempt of court but in California there is a specific statute which can extend the grounds on which a reporter can refuse to answer certain questions in a court of law.

The California statute is known as the Shield Law and it allows a journalist to keep confidential some facts pertaining to the methods used in compiling a story and events the reporter might have witnessed during the course of investigations. It was this law which Bashir and his ABC lawyers invoked when refusing to answer Mesereau's questions. Virtually every time the defence attorney posed a question, Bashir's lawyers objected. It got so ridiculous at one stage that it was agreed there could be a sort of running objection, so the repetition of the question-objection-ruling charade did not have to continue *ad infinitum*. The ultimate decision over whether a particular question falls under the protection afforded by the Shield Law is taken by the trial judge. In the Jackson case, the judge, Rodney Melville, allowed Bashir quite a large amount of latitude but there were four questions which Judge Melville ruled were admissible but which Bashir still refused to answer.

One question referred to Bashir's alleged misrepresentation. 'Did you get Michael Jackson to sign two documents without a lawyer present?' It is difficult to see why Bashir should find this so offensive. If there were no such documents, why not say so? If they existed, well, Jackson is an adult and Bashir cannot be held responsible if the singer freely chose to sign documents without a lawyer present. Not only that, Jackson had been a star surrounded by managers and attorneys since he was a toddler. If anyone knew the score, Jackson did. So what possible motive could Bashir have had for refusing to answer? Perhaps it was felt that opening this can of worms might expose what really goes on when reeling in a star for a television appearance. When the documentary was broadcast, Jackson said he felt 'betrayed' by Bashir. He claimed that Bashir promised to make a sympathetic film which would help turn the singer's life around. Another source supported the contention. The psychic, Uri Geller, who has been a long-time friend of Michael Jackson, said that both of them had been 'betrayed by Bashir'. It was like a re-run of the Diana imbroglio. For his part, Bashir denied all claims of 'distortion and misrepresentation levelled at me and the programme'.

The second question Bashir refused to answer was: 'How many hours of footage did you omit from the documentary?' Just why ABC's lawyers thought this question could fall under the Shield Law is not known but then again, the great broadcasting organisations would rather their viewers did not know that apparently real-time footage is, in fact, carefully edited. Mesereau then asked: 'Are you covering this case as a correspondent who is paid?' Again, there seems no obvious reason for Bashir to decline to respond. If he was not a working correspondent he could say so and in the process dismiss Mesereau's implication of a conflict of interest. If he was indeed covering the trial for ABC or anyone else, surely the jury had a right to know.

The strangest of all the refusals, though, was when Mesereau asked: 'Before this film was shown (to the court) and I am talking about the actual film shown by the prosecution today, did you watch the trial reel?' That question seems, at first glance, innocuous. Yet Bashir refused to tell the jury whether or not he had seen the film, despite Judge Melville's decision that the question did not fall under the Shield Law. Why would he do that? Only Bashir can actually say but it could be that the truthful response was 'no'. Bashir had either seen the reel or he hadn't. If he had, it seems inconceivable that he would not have let the court know. If he hadn't, that presented a serious problem for the prosecution. If Bashir had not seen the reel, then either the video screened in the court could not be proved to be exactly the same as the programme that was broadcast or it was the same but Bashir had never watched his own show, which was so unlikely as to be almost beyond mention. A 'current affairs film-maker', like any film-maker in any genre, would be derelict in his duty if he did not bother to watch the cut of his own programme. To my knowledge, no one has ever accused Bashir of that particular offence.

So can we safely assume that Bashir did watch his own programme? It would be extremely risky for Tom Sneddon and his team to have procured a video that was in any way different to that broadcast. It would be bound to be spotted by someone. And anyway, there was no point. The whole world had seen the programme and knew what was in it. A change, even a subtle one, would be spotted by the eagle-eyed defence team.

Chapter 2

The scenario that emerges from these considerations points to something else. In the prosecution's rush to get everything prepared for the opening of the trial and because Martin Bashir is an extremely busy person, he did not personally review the tape that was provided to the prosecution. If he had said this on the witness stand, the tape would not be authenticated and could not be used in evidence. Bashir was not about to lie on oath but if he admitted to not reviewing the tape, the prosecution's case would be in tatters. So, submerged in his other non-answers, he refused to answer this one. Bashir had given the impression publicly that he had no interest in Jackson being prosecuted. But in that case, why not just answer the question and allow the case to collapse? Perhaps Bashir was double-bluffing. On the one hand he wanted to be seen to be playing the role of good reporter by refusing to co-operate with the prosecution but actually he really wanted the prosecution to succeed. He certainly seemed annoyed and in bad temper with Tom Sneddon. Had something gone on behind the scenes which could have exonerated Michael Jackson but some deal had been hastily cobbled together to avert the collapse of the trial on its first day? To this day, that remains unanswered.

Judge Melville now had to decide what to do. Mesereau was on his feet, asking for all Bashir's evidence to be excluded but particularly the tape of *Living with Michael Jackson*. Although everyone knew the tape played was the actual programme, technically, it remained in part unauthenticated. It should have been thrown out. But it wasn't. If it had been the case might well have ended there and then. Instead, the learned judge said that he would rule on the matter later in the proceedings. For the moment, the tape was in. Although Mesereau continued throughout the trial to protest at the tape's inclusion, Judge Melville had no intention of ruling it out, and he didn't.

There still remained the question of what to do with the recalcitrant witness. Judge Melville had allowed Martin Bashir a certain amount of room to manoeuvre, ruling that the journalist need not answer a series of Mesereau's questions. However, Bashir had also refused to respond to some questions which the judge directed him to answer. This is contempt of court, pure and simple. Once again, Melville bottled it. Instead of citing Bashir for the obvious contempt, he again said he would rule on the matter later. So there was now the situation where two issues central to the case were in total confusion. Meanwhile, the trial continued as if the altercation had never happened. In the event no action was taken against Bashir. It was like the BBC all over again. If anyone 'got away with it' it wasn't Michael Jackson, it was Martin Bashir.

What are we to make of Martin Bashir in the trial of Michael Jackson? Although the vast majority of his actions can be seen in terms of journalistic endeavour, this does not entirely explain his contribution. Bashir's is a world where nothing can be taken at face value. It's a miasma of smoke and mirrors, a parallel universe where very little is real and image is all. The Jackson programme was undoubtedly helpful to the journalist's career. A few months after the trial, Bashir was made co-anchor of one of ABC News' most important current affairs shows, *Nightline*, taking over from the revered broadcaster, Ted Koppel, who was retiring. Fox News, not noted for its sympathy towards defendants in criminal trials, nevertheless was one of the few voices to question the appointment. Fox News reporter, Roger Friedman, was withering in his condemnation, saying: 'Congratulations, David Westin (the head of ABC News), you've replaced serious, competent, respected Ted Koppel with the oily, obsequious Martin Bashir on *Nightline*. My question is, was Jerry Springer not available?' Friedman then went even further, with the claim that 'His (Bashir's) method of getting headline-making answers is as dishonest as it could possibly be.' This last comment referred to the outtakes of *Living with Michael Jackson* which were shown to the court. According to Friedman's analysis, Bashir 'baits Jackson, praising his strangest qualities during breaks in filming. Jackson is flattered and pleased but when filming resumes Bashir then attacks the singer for the traits he, only seconds earlier, complimented.'

While there was nothing in *Living with Michael Jackson* to prove criminality on the part of the singer, just like Bashir's programme on Terry Venables, there was just enough ammunition to entice others into the fray, some far more sinister than Martin Bashir.

3

THE MAD DOG BITES

By 2003, the predators had been gathering around Michael Jackson for some years. There were numerous civil lawsuits, most relating to disputes between the singer and various colleagues-turned-adversaries, arising from Jackson's activities in the music industry. There was also any number of ex-employees claiming a variety of grievances. One litigant, for instance, was a concert promoter called Marcel Avram, who filed two such cases against Jackson, one for $20 million dollars that was settled for somewhat less than the amount claimed, followed immediately by another, this time for a mere $5 million. Although Michael Jackson has been involved in hundreds of law-suits or potential law-suits over the years – the vast majority of them bogus – a qualitative difference had occurred over the previous decade. More legal suits against Jackson were succeeding (or he settled the cases out of court) and as the singer's career suffered during the 1990s, the litigation increased. But the man who saw himself as Jackson's nemesis had no connection to the record business, nor was he a disgruntled former employee. He was the District Attorney of Santa Barbara County in California. Thwarted ten years earlier in his attempt to convict Michael Jackson of child sexual abuse, after *Living with Michael Jackson* hit the world's television screens, Thomas W. Sneddon Jr believed his chance for payback had finally arrived.

In fact, Tom Sneddon does have a connection to the music industry. He is widely believed to be the inspiration for the Michael Jackson song, 'D.S.', which appeared on the 'HIStory' album of 1996. Not many of us can say that.

The song rubbed salt into the wounds Sneddon sustained when he failed to force Jackson into court in 1994. In Jackson's version of *Citizen Kane*, Randoph Hearst becomes Tom Sneddon. Sneddon is then given the name Dom Sheldon. Sheldon, according to the song, leads a conspiracy that is out to destroy Michael Jackson. 'They wanna get my ass dead or

35

alive. You know he really tried to take me down by surprise,' go the lyrics. When Tom Sneddon opened his new investigation into Jackson in 2003, the media were quick to remind the public about this song. They treated it as something of a joke, as did Sneddon when asked about his reaction to it. 'I have not, shall we say, done him the honour of listening to it but I've been told that it ends with the sound of a gunshot,' he said. In contrast to the frivolity of the public discourse, Michael Jackson was deadly serious and believed every word of that song.

Tom Sneddon hails from Los Angeles, where his father was a baker. Sneddon Jr attended the university of Notre Dame, soon becoming known for his prowess as an athlete, particularly in the boxing ring. Having gone on to study law at UCLA he spent a tour of duty in Vietnam for two years with the US army. Upon his return home he entered the law full-time, eventually heading north to Santa Barbara as an assistant DA. In the late seventies he assumed responsibility for the Criminal Operations Division and by the 1980s had developed such a reputation he was taken seriously as a potential candidate for District Attorney. In 1986 he ran for election to the top job and won. Since that first contest, he has been re-elected unopposed every time his term of office was up, in the process becoming Santa Barbara's longest serving DA.

Normally, when a lawyer joins the exalted ranks of elected district attorneys his or her career trajectory shifts from criminal prosecutor to politician. All the prosecutors in the OJ Simpson case, for instance, were assistant DA's. The LA District Attorney, Gil Garcetti, no longer advocates in court unless there are very specific circumstances. Sneddon runs an operation in Santa Barbara where he has to oversee a staff which includes nearly 250 prosecutors. Any one of them might make a wrong decision which could affect public opinion and threaten the DA's chances at the next election. Running the show and setting policy is a full-time job in itself. Sneddon is unusual in that he still prosecutes cases himself. Not any old cases, of course. His position allows him to pick and choose.

During his time as a full-time prosecutor, Sneddon became known for his combativeness in and out of the courtroom, hence his nickname, 'Mad Dog'. The editor of one of the local newspapers, the Santa Barbara News Press' Jerry Roberts, described Sneddon as 'pugnacious and tenacious, he has a reputation for being fiercely competitive.' Sneddon himself recognised this when he said: 'I've been in this business now for thirty-three years. So clearly, there were times when I was probably developing my skills and personality in the courtroom and maybe at times wasn't as controlled as I am now.'

There is at least one person in Santa Barbara who does not believe in the new, mellow, Tom Sneddon. He is a defence attorney known as Gary – or sometimes Dennis – Dunlap. Dunlap has been a thorn in the side of the Santa Barbara DA's office for some time, criticising the District Attorney's methods and motives. That put him on Tom Sneddon's hit list. He was accused of perjury and witness intimidation, extremely serious charges carrying a penalty of many years in jail. Dunlap, in an understandably bitter outburst in 2003, said: 'Last year (2002) I was wrongfully prosecuted (by Sneddon) for a number of crimes, crimes I did not commit. We went to a jury trial and I was acquitted on all counts.' Declaring that he would sue Sneddon for malicious prosecution, Dunlap took a sideswipe at the DA, saying, 'He said he had a very strong case against me. The problem was that his whole strong case was manufactured.'

Tom Sneddon has also taken a keen interest in family-law cases over the years. This is not surprising given that he has nine children (including one set of twins) of his own. Moreover, he is part of the religious conservative right in the USA's ongoing culture wars, particularly on 'family' issues. In 1991 a new section of his office was formed called Child Support Enforcement and Sneddon was appointed chair. Two years later, an opportunity occurred to turn his interest in the worthy but mundane area of child support into a full-blown and sensational criminal trial.

Sneddon first crossed swords with Michael Jackson in 1993, when he started an investigation into allegations of sexual abuse brought against Jackson by Jordan Chandler, or more accurately, Jordan's father, Evan. Jordan Chandler had met Michael Jackson fleetingly on a couple of occasions as a youngster. He was a Michael Jackson fan, like millions throughout the world. On a fateful day in May 1992, when Jordan was twelve, Michael Jackson's car broke down in Los Angeles. Jordan's step-father, Dave Schwartz, owned a car-rental company and was on hand to sort out Jackson's transportation problems. That chance encounter was to change the lives of all those present that day and many more.

Schwartz called his wife, June, who was Jordan's mother, and asked her to hurry and come to the nearby car rental office. He told her to bring Jordan with her. That was when and where Jordan Chandler met Michael

Jackson. Those facts are agreed. Just about everything that occurred thereafter, however, including whether or not the pop star groomed then molested the boy, has been argued over, spun and interpreted to oblivion: except in a court of law.

I reviewed most of the literature surrounding the Chandler-Jackson tragedy. What struck me were the terrible effects the case had on everyone involved. Nobody won. Nobody was vindicated. The Chandlers were effectively destroyed as a family. Michael Jackson's career and the way he was perceived by a once-adoring public were tainted beyond repair. Even many of the lawyers saw their reputations severely damaged. One protagonist, a Los Angeles private detective called Anthony Pellicano, who worked sporadically for Jackson and whose behaviour in the case was questionable to say the least, saw his lucrative career, which was based on sorting out damaging problems for the stars, nosedive. At the time of writing he is in jail, having been convicted of a number of serious charges including possession of guns and explosives. And the case continues to haunt the other participants like the curse of Tutankhamun. It possesses the restless energy of a tidal wave, cascading down the years and forever retaining its power to swamp and overwhelm.

The most comprehensive accounts of the debacle are contained in two books. The updated edition of J. Randy Taraborrelli's excellent biography, *Michael Jackson: The Magic and the Madness*, is so good it can make you totally believe Jackson did it at one point, then be equally convinced of his innocence the next. Thus it can claim more neutrality than most. It does present much evidence and its early edition has remained the definitive account of Jackson's life. Yet if someone as knowledgeable and skilled as Taraborrelli has difficulty in deciding the truth of the matter, what chance do the rest of us have?

The book *All That Glitters* by Jordan Chandler's uncle (his father's brother), Raymond Chandler, was published in 2004, ten years after the events it describes and at the time when the consequences of *Living with Michael Jackson* were gathering momentum by the day. It has a sad tale to tell. Raymond Chandler is undoubtedly biased (he is convinced Jackson did it) but he puts forward facts and motivations that have not previously been aired. The author also convinces me that he sincerely wishes to use his experience to do something positive about the problem of child abuse.

So, in *All That Glitters*, Chandler gives us the details surrounding the main evidence against Jackson, including Jordan Chandler's statements, especially those he made to child-abuse experts. Indeed, *All That Glitters*, like the law enforcement agencies involved at the time, makes much of the experts' opinions that Jordan's allegations were true. However, the opinions of child-abuse experts have been shown to be less than infallible in the intervening years. Many ordinary families have been needlessly and recklessly torn asunder by experts proclaiming such outrages as Satanic Abuse and Repressed Memory Syndrome, both found later to be beset with profound difficulties, if they exist at all. So while the opinions of experts in this field should carry weight, they can no longer be conclusive proof in of abuse in themselves. Chandler makes no mention of these developments in his book.

There is, however, something that appears in both books which is extremely illuminating. The initial complaint against Michael Jackson was made to the children's authorities in Los Angeles. The matter was further investigated by the Los Angeles Police department (LAPD) and at an early stage the Los Angeles District Attorney's office was the leading agency in terms of mounting a criminal prosecution. But Gil Garcetti never authorised a trial.

Each book gives its own account of the prosecutorial process. While the emphasis differs the story is essentially the same: Garcetti's procrastination. Nevertheless, they don't agree on the reason for Garcetti's eventual decision. According to Taraborrelli, it was (so Jackson's camp thought) because the DA had lost a number of high-profile cases, including the acquittal of police officers who had beaten up Rodney King and the deadlocked jury in the first trial of the Menendez brothers, who killed their own parents. This made Garcetti wary of taking on a world star with the resources to present a credible defence. In Chandler's book, Garcetti's thinking becomes a manifestation of out-and-out dirty politics: the DA knew Jackson did it but was afraid of alienating the electorate, who might see any prosecution as celebrity-hounding and thus lead to the polarisation of voters. That could jeopardise Garcetti's chances of re-election. Taraborrelli also gives an alternative view: that there were some in Garcetti's department who thought Michael Jackson might be innocent, or at least not guilty beyond a reasonable doubt.

If *All That Glitters* is to be believed, there were other jurisdictions where abuse against Jordan Chandler took place, from Monaco to New York and Las Vegas. None of the authorities in any of these locations saw fit to mount an investigation, let alone a prosecution. However, no such thoughts inhibited Tom Sneddon in his pursuit of the suspected child abuser, Michael Jackson. Indeed, Sneddon gave the impression of relishing the contest.

During the course of the investigation in 1994, Sneddon ordered Jackson to undergo a humiliating procedure. The star was stripped of his clothes and had his genitalia photographed. Sneddon's justification for this was that he needed visual evidence to corroborate Jordan Chandler's description of the intimate parts of Jackson's anatomy. The singer was unsurprisingly extremely upset by the ordeal. Although Sneddon was able to put some legal gloss on his attempts go get Jackson photographed naked, the process became something of a stunt. Any evidentiary value the photos may have contained – which was always questionable – was overtaken by a further frenzy over the possibility that the pictures would find their way into the public domain.

Much has been written about the case of Michael Jackson and Jordan Chandler. Even more was read into Jackson's decision to pay Chandler a huge sum of money rather than fight the boy's allegations in court. Whether or not Jackson committed any criminal offence remains unknown because there was never any trial at which the evidence could be tested. We are left with various assertions. Jackson came under intense pressure to settle the case, especially from his management and his record label, Sony, not because they thought he was guilty, but for commercial considerations whatever the outcome of a court case might have been. They believed that even if a criminal trial resulted in a not guilty verdict, severe damage would be inflicted on Jackson's career, with massive financial consequences for themselves. It must also be said that many of them, particularly at Sony, felt Jackson was guilty. What they failed to realise was that a settlement, while not legally an admission of guilt, is nevertheless regarded as such by large sections of the public and most of the media.

When considering a person's reputation, and I refer here to someone who is publicly known, truth often takes a back seat. It is the spin that shapes the perception. Take the case of Che Guevara, one of the great revolutionaries of the twentieth century, whose picture adorns the most popular poster of all time and appears on millions of T-shirts from Boston to Bombay.

Ernesto 'Che' Guevara cuts a romantic figure across the generations. His place in the public's affections stems from the time in the 1950s, when, at the side of Fidel Castro, he helped defeat the mighty forces running Cuba (the Batista government supported by the USA and funded by the mafia). Guevara was thus instrumental in effecting the Cuban Revolution, which, of course, has lasted to the present day, despite the best efforts of ten US Presidents. When Guevara left Cuba at the height of his powers to export the revolution to other parts of the world his reputation grew. When he died in Bolivia while fighting for his version of socialism, his position was sealed. People related to a man who fought and died for what he believed in, even if they didn't agree with his politics.

Yet Che Guevara was responsible for the deaths of many hundreds, if not thousands of people, both in the Revolutionary Courts he established in Cuba after he and Castro took power and later in the wars of liberation he fought in Africa and Latin America. This was brought home to me when I met a girl in Miami in the 1970s whose parents had been killed in the early days of Guevara's courts. Nevertheless, Che remains a revered figure. I even made a tiny contribution myself to his legend when I wrote an article for the left wing UK magazine, *Red Pepper*, exposing the way in which the Kennedy administration spurned Guevara's offer of a *modus vivendi* with Cuba at a meeting with one of the late President's most trusted aides, Richard Goodwin, in Punta del Este, Chile, in the early sixties and how this ushered in the instigation of 'Operation Mongoose', which sought to destabilise Cuba and assassinate Fidel Castro.

Michael Jackson has not killed anyone as far as I am aware. Yet his reputation is in tatters while Guevara's goes from strength to strength. I am not seeking here to make a comparison between the two or enter into a dialectic about the merits or otherwise of Guevara's life, far from it. I am merely trying to illustrate how spin and propaganda can influence how we view those in the public eye.

The political also works at the personal level. During the early 1990s I wanted to write an article on a remarkable youth football team which was touring England. They were called Tahuichi and they came from Bolivia, one of the poorest countries in the southern hemisphere. In the course of my research I was invited to the Bolivian Embassy in London where I was introduced to the ambassador, Gary Prado Salmón. Sr. Prado and I later became great friends. On one occasion, after we had finished our football discussions, Prado told me something of his life. As a General in the Bolivian army he had lost the use of his legs after being shot while trying to bring a dispute between warring factions to a peaceful conclusion. But it was a story from much earlier in his career, when he was an army captain, which made the most impression on me. In 1967, he led the force which captured, then killed, Che Guevara.

Prado told me that after the skirmish which led to Che's capture, he arranged for Guevara to spend what turned out to be the revolutionary's last night on this earth as a prisoner in a schoolhouse in a small village in rural Bolivia. During the course of the evening Prado and Guevara had a long and detailed conversation about world politics and the situation in Bolivia. From being a typical army man who believed in the system that was at the time in place in his country, Prado told me how the fervour and force of Guevara's arguments left a deep impression upon him. Many years later, Prado was one of the leading figures who brought democracy to his blighted country and he told me how that conversation with Che Guevara influenced his thinking in that direction. There were tears in eyes when he recounted how, on the morning following Che Guevara's capture, he received orders from the capital, La Paz, to lead a small force to mop up the rest of Guevara's band of revolutionaries. He knew there were no guerrillas left to mop up and wondered why he had been given such a command. But orders are orders and he did as he was directed. When he returned to the village, he saw that it was now in the control of the US Central Intelligence Agency, and Guevara had been shot dead.

The point of this story is that nothing is black and white. There are always shades of grey. But perception, as George Orwell understood when he invented the word 'Newspeak' in his novel, *1984*, to describe a partic-ular form of propaganda where the meaning and usage of words is twisted to fit the requirements of a ruling elite, is everything. Latin American general or dead revolutionary! Image says one is a hideous fascist, while the other a role model. Nothing could be further from the truth. If anything, in today's world, it has to be even more simple. If you are not for us, you are against us.

Settling the Chandler case out of court turned out to be disastrous for Michael Jackson. It turned him into something of a pariah, despite there being no trial at which he could be found guilty or not. Part of the problems lay with Jackson's presentation of himself. Over many years, he used his superstar status to put himself on a moral pedestal. He was like Jesus and Mother Theresa rolled into one. Any hint of a fall from grace and he was damaged goods. His diehard fans always maintained their loyalty by refusing to believe Jackson could ever do anything wrong. It was necessary not to entertain even a scintilla of doubt. For the rest of the world, the case knocked Michael Jackson off his throne and for the King of Pop that would eventually prove terminal. By settling with Jordan Chandler, particularly for the very public amount of $20 million, the catastrophe the settlement was supposed to avert was actually brought about.

Still, in the end it was Michael Jackson's decision. We now know that it was a no-win situation. When accused of certain crimes, of which child sex abuse is a prominent example, if the defendant settles, he's guilty. If he fights and wins in a court of law – he's still guilty and in the meantime much damaging evidence might have emerged. There is no room here for the possibility of innocence. Consequently, although Tom Sneddon felt cheated out of his due reward of a guilty verdict against Jackson in court, he nevertheless helped precipitate the star's spectacular downfall. The fact is, Jackson's career never really recovered from Jordan Chandler's allegations and the way Tom Sneddon investigated the case. Or perhaps it was on the brink of recovery when *Living with Michael Jackson* struck with the explosive power of a cruise missile.

The law as it stood in California at the time allowed Jordan Chandler not to testify in any criminal proceedings against the singer once a civil settlement between the two was agreed. This was a blow to Tom Sneddon, who had been convinced that if no one else would do it, he would be the one to bring Jackson to trial. He had, he said, a 'strong case'. So annoyed was he that Jackson had slipped through his fingers, he lent his considerable weight to a successful campaign to get the law changed. Today, a settlement agreement in a civil case cannot include an obligation on any party not to testify in a criminal case. So when *Living with Michael Jackson* was aired in 2003, there is a story that a number of people in the Santa Barbara prosecutor's office punched the air in delight.

Seemingly unable to put the Chandler case behind him, Tom Sneddon was straining at the leash to resume his pursuit of Michael Jackson. He told *Vanity Fair* in 1995 that his investigation into the Jordan Chandler allegations was not closed but was 'in suspension'. Sneddon sounded like a man bent on revenge. However, he faced a number of problems in the new situation that occurred in 2003. For instance, there was no victim making accusations, merely a television programme which neither showed nor admitted any criminal wrongdoing on Jackson's part. All Sneddon had to go on was a display of physical closeness between Michael Jackson and Gavin Arvizo, plus a statement by Jackson that offered up the fact that he slept in the same bedroom as the boy. Moreover, the star denied any sexual content in his relationships with children. There was, however, a lot of public and media outrage.

The force of the storm that broke after the broadcast of *Living with Michael Jackson* was fuelled by public pronouncements from child welfare experts. Within days and without conducting any interviews with those involved, one of these experts, Dr Carole Lieberman, wrote letters of complaint to the authorities in Los Angeles and Santa Barbara. Before long she was issuing statements to the media. She was intervening, she claimed, because others were 'standing by and letting these children be potentially harmed'. In response to Dr Lieberman and others who wrote similar letters of complaint, Tom Sneddon appeared cautious. What we witnessed on television was, he said, 'no substitute for credible, co-operative victims'. Some took Sneddon's remark to mean that he was not planning any new investigation into Michael Jackson. In fact, Sneddon's comments were a smoke screen. What he actually meant was that he was about to devote all the resources he could muster to ensure that Gavin Arvizo was the victim he required. By the middle of February 2003, at Sneddon's urging, the Santa Barbara Sheriff began to conduct an enquiry into the affair. In keeping with the false impression Tom Sneddon's statement had created, the Sheriff's investigation was not made public.

No such Machiavellian intrigue surrounded the operations of the Los Angeles Department of Child and Family Services (DCFS) when they looked into the matter at about the same time as the Santa Barbara Sheriff. After interviewing the relevant parties, including Gavin Arvizo, the DCFS decided that any allegations of abuse were 'unfounded' and closed the case. Similarly, the LAPD, after a short investigation, decided there was insufficient evidence to proceed. In the face of these conclusions even the Santa Barbara Sheriff was deterred. Internal documents produced by the Sheriff's department revealed that 'the elements of criminal intent (necessary for a successful prosecution) were not met.' The reason why three separate investigating authorities reached the same conclusion was that Gavin Arvizo, supported by his family members, claimed he had never been abused by Michael Jackson. On the contrary, the young Arvizo went to great lengths to portray his relationship with the singer as non-sexual. He did not simply deny any wrongdoing by Jackson. He said, among many positive statements, that the star was 'like a father' to him. Undaunted by these reverses, 'Mad Dog' Sneddon pressed on. There was going to be a re-match with Michael Jackson. Tom Sneddon, the college sports star, knew all about re-matches. This time he would win.

Over the course of the next few months, Sneddon developed what was to prove a complicated (and ultimately unsuccessful) strategy. First, it would be necessary to question the exoneration of Jackson by various law enforcement agencies, particularly the DCFS. A whispering campaign against the DCFS began which pointed to 'problems' in the organisation, although the exact nature of these problems was never specified. The tactic culminated when, at the press conference on the eve of Michael Jackson's arrest, Sneddon really laid into the DCFS, saying, 'To call that (the DCFS enquiry) an investigation is a misnomer. It was an interview … that's all it was.' Sneddon's comments were disingenuous to say the least. All investigations rely on interviews and an interpretation of what has been said. If the DCFS had conducted the same interviews but reached the opposite conclusion there is no doubt that Sneddon would have used the subsequent report to justify charges. Tom Sneddon, however, had a higher purpose and no one, not even his law enforcement colleagues, would be allowed to stand in his way if they disagreed with his decisions. Of course, Sneddon did not mention the fact that his own Santa Barbara Sheriff's office had reached the same conclusion as the DCFS. He didn't need to because the Sheriff's enquiry was carried out in secret.

The next step for Sneddon was to detach the Arvizo family from Jackson. This objective was accomplished by a combination of stick and carrot. The stick was contained in threats to prosecute Janet Arvizo (Gavin's mother) for welfare fraud and investigate her behaviour in a court action against a store chain for injuries and sexual harassment she claimed she sustained during a dispute with the store's security men in a car park. The carrot for the Arvizos was that a successful criminal prosecution against Jackson for molesting Gavin could lead to a multi-million dollar civil suit against the star. Quite simply, staying in Jackson's corner would lead the Arvizos nowhere except towards further dependence on the singer. Testify against him and they could all be rich.

Once the Arvizo-Jackson axis had been split, it was imperative that Sneddon get all the family, especially Gavin, to admit that abuse of Gavin by Michael Jackson had taken place. In addition, any admissions had to be usable. That is, they had to be able to result in credible testimony in court and as far as possible put forward plausible reasons for the earlier denials. If Sneddon achieved these objectives he had a good chance of securing a conviction. Whether his actions served the truth only he can say.

Precisely why the Arvizos moved one hundred and eighty degrees, from fulsome supporters of Michael Jackson to dangerous adversaries, is a question which eludes a conclusive answer. According to the version put forward by Tom Sneddon and the Arvizos in court, Jackson's entourage had kept them incommunicado after the US broadcast of *Living with Michael Jackson*. Furthermore, the story went, they had been coerced into denying any molestation by the singer and had even been supplied a script to use in Jackson's rebuttal video of Martin Bashir's programme. They even went so far as to say that Jackson tried to spirit them out of the country to Brazil. Eventually they were able to escape Jackson's clutches and seek sanctuary in the ample arms of District Attorney Sneddon. Once free, they claimed, they could reveal the true story.

It was these allegations that formed the basis of the charge of conspiracy which was later brought against Jackson. By its nature, one person alone cannot engage in a conspiracy. However, no one else was ever charged in connection with this alleged conspiracy. The legal jargon is phrased in conspiracy cases to take account of this. When someone is charged it says the conspiratorial behaviour took place either with named individuals or 'person or persons unknown'. In the Jackson case, the Arvizos named the people they said had kept them prisoners and forced them to comply with the making of the rebuttal video. So the others in the conspiracy could not have been unknown. Tom Sneddon has never been called to account for this anomaly at the heart of his case.

As you would expect, Michael Jackson's criminal defence attorney at trial, Tom Mesereau, had a completely different story to tell. The Arvizos, in particular the mother, Janet, were money-grabbing scam-artists, trying to screw as much as they possibly could out of an innocent man. When their chance came, after the screening of *Living with Michael Jackson*, they turned on their benefactor by colluding with the DA in telling the court a pack of lies. Janet Arvizo was so dastardly, Mesereau observed, that she was even prepared to use her young children to further her abominable plan.

J. Randy Taraborrelli, in his updated edition of *Michael Jackson: The Magic & the Madness*, suggests that soon after *Living with Michael Jackson* was broadcast the singer's advisors brought in the high-profile defence attorney, Mark Geragos, to fight Jackson's corner. At the time, Jackson himself refused to deal with the problems created by Bashir's documentary. Geragos, being the good lawyer he is, immediately advised Jackson to distance himself from the Arvizos, especially Gavin. By how far Geragos' advice was implemented when Janet Arvizo began to feel nervous about the way things were turning out has been the subject of much speculation. What is known is that she eventually found her way to Larry Feldman, the attorney who had helped Jordan Chandler to relieve Michael Jackson of some $20 million in 1994. And lurking, awaiting his opportunity to strike was the Mad Dog. Thus did the Arvizo family pass from one protector, Michael Jackson, to another, Tom Sneddon, like some feudal chattel. Many would think that was as clear a case of 'out of the frying pan, into the fire' as you could get.

Once Sneddon had ensnared the Arvizos, a steady stream of stories began to circulate to the effect that Gavin Arvizo had changed his position and abuse was definitely now being alleged. Slowly, the DA began to turn up the heat on his quarry.

Over the next few months Sneddon developed his case against Jackson. He had to jump through a number of hoops to do so as there was always a question mark against the truthfulness of the Arvizo family. The DA hoped to find incriminating evidence at Neverland and conducted a series of high-profile searches of the property. When the raids yielded little of value, apart from some soft-core material which might be available in half of all US households and was entirely legal, Sneddon embarked on an extraordinary course of action. He decided to charge Jackson with molesting Gavin Arvizo, but claimed the abuse took place after the broadcast of *Living with Michael Jackson*. To hedge his bets, he also appealed publicly for anyone else to come forward if they alleged that Michael Jackson had molested them. As fishing expeditions go, this was a humdinger.

This amazing turn of events has drawn widespread comment, as has Sneddon's associated decision to charge Jackson with conspiracy to falsely imprison the Arvizos after *Living with Michael Jackson* rudely interrupted their world. For our purposes it is sufficient to say that Sneddon's behaviour betrayed a determination bordering on pathological obsession.

In the middle of all this, Tom Sneddon received some exclusive information. Although at first sight it appeared tangential to his investigations, it was something Sneddon decided was dynamite, the missing piece of his evidential jigsaw. The King of Pop was gonna take a fall. Sneddon had no doubt about that now. The tip-off he received came via New York but had ultimately been formulated and sanctioned thousands of miles away, in Tokyo.

4

VERY DEVILISH

On a lovely sunny day in May 2002 an extraordinary sequence of events took place in the centre of Manhattan. A rally was being held to promote the unusual cause of artists' rights and Revd Al Sharpton, the firebrand preacher and civil rights activist (and sometime actor), was the key speaker. The gathering drew widespread media attention, particularly when Michael Jackson showed up to participate in what was supposed to be a protest against the huge corporate entities which these days control the music and entertainment industries. At one point, a motorcade, including Jackson in an open-top bus, stopped outside the headquarters of the Sony Corporation, the old, imposing AT&T building occupying a whole block on the west side of Madison Avenue in midtown between 54th and 55th streets.

As the throng began chanting abuse in the general direction of Sony's offices, staff inside were astonished to see the King of Pop, who was, after all, one of their own, very well-remunerated artists, leading the protest. They were even more amazed when a placard was held up bearing the slogan, 'Go back to hell, Tommy'. The Tommy being referred to was Tommy Mottola, head of Sony's US record division. While Mottola was not the most popular record company executive in the world, those working inside the building simply couldn't comprehend what was going on. One of them told me they 'dismissed it as a joke. It just showed that Michael (Jackson) had finally lost it. Mind you, we were talking about it for weeks.'

Although rallies in support of rich pop stars are not commonplace in New York (or anywhere else for that matter), in itself it was uncontroversial. That is until Michael Jackson decided to involve himself in the proceedings. If the placard were not enough, Jackson upped the ante considerably when he took the speaker's microphone at a press conference to promote the rally. At that moment, the event was turned from a publicity offensive against multi-national corporations run by accountants and lawyers to the

49

Michael Jackson show. 'Tommy Mottola,' Jackson said, 'is mean, racist and very, very devilish'.

These words travelled around the world in double-quick time. However, they were, in the main, misunderstood. Newspapers, radio stations and television networks decided as one that Michael Jackson calling Mottola a racist was the sensational bit so they concentrated on that. Soon, the world remembered only the racist insult. Earnest debates took place on radio, television and the internet. Those who knew Tommy Mottola said he might be many things but racist was not one of them. Others used the spat to point out that racism is still endemic in the world of entertainment.

The back-story the media spun to support their reporting was that Jackson, annoyed at the relative failure of his CD *Invincible*, blamed the poor sales (any other artist would covet the success of *Invincible*, which sold more than 20 million copies worldwide) on Sony in general and Tommy Mottola in particular, thus Jackson's statement was personal and driven by self-interest. That served to focus minds on the racist issue but it could also be dismissed as a 'weird Jacko' rant. Whether the media's reporting had any positive effects on the issue of racism in the music business – which is as important today as it ever was – is open to question. But none of that was what Michael Jackson meant to convey.

When reading the words spoken by Jackson at the rally it is natural to go along with the media's interpretation of the central allegation: Tommy Mottola, according to Michael Jackson, is a racist. However, watching Jackson actually speaking the sentence gives a very different impression. 'Mean' and 'racist' appear for introductory purposes or perhaps as throw-away insults intended to give advance warning of what Jackson was actually trying to say. There can be no doubt that the most important part of Jackson's statement as far as he was concerned, comes at the end, when he accuses Mottola of being 'very, very devilish'.

It is the case that Michael Jackson believed Sony had not been marketing his records properly for some time but this alone did not provide the motivation for his outburst. Since signing a famous, ten to fifteen-year, so-called $1 billion dollar contract in 1991, he had become ever more disillusioned in his relationship with his record label. That deal came hard on the heels of Tommy Mottola convincing Jackson to support him in his battle to take over the job of his then boss, Walter Yetnikoff, as head of the US record label. It was Jackson's support for Mottola that swayed Sony's Japanese leadership in their decision to take Mottola's side against Yetnikoff. Michael Jackson knew he was instrumental in Mottola's promotion. Yet now Mottola, far from redeeming his promises to give Jackson's career fresh impetus, was repaying his debt by abandoning the singer in favour of other artists.

Jackson was also going much further, implying that Tommy Mottola was actively engaged in an attempt to sabotage his, Jackson's, career, hence the use of the word 'devilish'. Michael Jackson had no idea how close he was to the truth yet how far away he was from understanding the reality of what was occurring. He thought it was about CD sales and marketing. It was actually about survival.

Michael Jackson became entangled with the Sony Corporation almost by accident. When the Jackson 5 left Motown in the mid 1970s, the label they signed to was not Sony but Columbia Broadcasting Systems (CBS), one of America's most prestigious companies. CBS made its name as an early pioneer of radio services in the 1930s and over the next five decades – under the leadership of the legendary entrepreneur, William Paley – developed into one of the world's premier broadcasting organisations. Not only that, it was known even beyond its own shores for its commitment to high-quality news programming. Moreover, the CBS correspondent and news anchor, Walter Cronkite, was known the world over for the integrity of his broadcasts, particularly during the Vietnam war. CBS's record division was similarly blue chip, having been a major force in the American record industry for many years. When the Jackson 5 joined the label, its roster included the likes of Barbra Streisand, Bob Dylan, The O'Jays and the Three Degrees. In the future there would be Bruce Springsteen, George Michael and many, many others. CBS branded its first label *Columbia*, later adding a more youthful counterpart, *Epic*.

Sony completed the takeover of CBS Records in January 1988. By then, Michael Jackson was basking in the success of 'Thriller' and 'Bad' and was the biggest superstar on the planet. It would not be too fanciful to suggest that Jackson was one of the main reasons Sony bought CBS when it did. The purchase was the first step in a plan devised by the Japanese corporation, the ultimate aim of which was massively to diversify Sony's global activities. Already the world leader in the design and manufacture of consumer electronics, the Japanese behemoth was, by the end of the 1980s, poised to conquer the world of entertainment. After all, if you've invented the Walkman, why not own the music played on it?

Chapter 4

The existing CBS management in all territories was not only retained, many of its top executives were paid handsome bonuses to continue to work for the new corporation, Sony Music (the company was renamed Sony Music Entertainment after the acquisition of Columbia Pictures in 1989). The record label was left in the CBS building, built by Paley as a monument to CBS's success and known to everyone as Black Rock, due its cladding of Canadian granite. Situated on the Avenue of the Americas between 52nd and 53rd streets, the thirty-five storey monolith was designed by renowned architect, Eero Saarinen. Four years after the takeover, the record label was moved to Sony's head office on Madison Avenue.

Although Sony had been in the record business in Japan for many years – it had been part of a joint venture with CBS since 1968 – the corporation had no real knowledge of how to run an international record label. And anyway, those running the CBS operation, particularly Walter Yetnikoff in New York and Paul Russell in London, had delivered a spectacular series of performances throughout the 1980s, with huge turnover and profits. At the pinnacle of this revenue-generating machine Sony now owned was, of course, the man who had produced the biggest selling record of all time, Michael Jackson.

Yetnikoff, who according to a close colleague was 'the greatest artist-relations man in the business', was dispatched to ensure Jackson was onside with the takeover. Yetnikoff had been looking after Jackson on behalf of CBS for many years so the singer and the record executive had built a good relationship during that time. Yetnikoff told Jackson that things would not simply remain the same now Sony had bought CBS, they would be better. At last, Yetnikoff said, they wouldn't have to suffer the pettifogging interferences of the CBS board, which was always fearful of the record division doing something that might result in a scandal and jeopardise the company's precious federal licences to operate its television network. Jackson bought Yetnikoff's hard-sell. It was to prove a fateful decision.

The Sony Corporation's roots lie in strange soil. The official history states that the company was incorporated in Tokyo on 7 May 1946 as Tokyo Tsushin Kogyo (Tokyo Telecommunications (and) Engineering Corporation). It was more commonly known as Totsuko. Over a decade later, when the company was far more established, the founding fathers, Akio Morita and Masaru Ibuka, changed its name to Sony, which had been used as a product brand name for three years. Apparently, the name was intended to symbolise Sonus (Latin for sound) and the diminutive of son (in English, sonny). It seems to me far more likely that as the company internationalised in the 1950s, especially after the technology to produce cheap transistors was developed and they were getting ready for flotation on the Tokyo stock exchange, Morita wanted a less Japanese sounding name. It must be admitted, though, that Morita, who was a fervent nationalist and champion of the new Japan, did not wish to discard all connections between the corporate brand name and his homeland. Hence the invention of a word – Sony – not contained in any language as far as I know and therefore acceptable to international ears. The cleverness of the new name went further. The word, or something like it, was used at the time in Japanese colloquial speech to describe a smiling (male) child.

Akio Morita's patriotism was not confined to his support for the new society created in the wake of the military defeat of 1945. He was, for example, a firm believer in the potential of both the Japanese character and the nation's culture. Before the war, like all young Japanese, he was a devotee of the imperial project and during that period his nationalism was directed towards worship of the emperor and lauding the country's military prowess and martial history. Morita graduated as one of the best engineers of his generation. He was also a great organiser. It was not surprising, therefore, that he put his expertise at the disposal of the regime and became a central figure in a secret wartime military programme directed against the United States.

The innocuous-sounding Precision Instrument and Research Committee (PIRC) was, in fact, engaged in advanced weapons research, the results of which, it was hoped at the time, would inflict serious damage on the USA's war effort. The technological miracle that occurred in Japan after the war did not come out of the blue. The young engineer-scientists of PIRC concentrated on producing guidance systems, for example, which involved a degree of miniaturisation which did not exist before they got to work. It was also important to be able to mass produce cheaply any weapons systems they developed. Only by doing this could Japan hope to compete with the production capability of the Americans, who could turn out a warship a week during the height of the conflict. PIRC was also tasked with designing delivery systems for chemical and biological agents, and developing computerisation for rockets and other weaponry.

Many of those engaged in intelligence analysis during the Second World War who are still alive, believe that Japan received information from Germany on the production of atomic power for an explosive device. It is true that Germany's atomic scientists worked on a programme using uranium originating in the Congo but seized by the Nazis when they occupied Belgium, and heavy water from hydroelectric power generation plants in Norway. It is also the case that when Hitler began to cool on paying the costs of atomic development and the Norwegian facility came under attack from the allies, it affected the Japanese perspective more than the other axis powers as they were not entirely without knowledge of American efforts to build an atomic device. It is therefore at least possible that, in addition to the conventional weapons research going on at PIRC, Akio Morita, future head of Sony, had some input into exploring ways of blowing the USA to kingdom come. The whole PIRC project came to an abrupt halt with the surrender of Japan after the detonation of two American atomic bombs at Hiroshima and Nagasaki in 1945. .

Despite extensive conventional bombing of the industrial parts of Japan by the Americans during the war, PIRC's facilities somehow remained undamaged. The tightly-knit group of technicians who were essential to the core activities of PIRC also survived and came to see themselves as Japan's very own Band of Brothers. Led by Akio Morita, they stuck together to further their new objective: rebuilding Japan from the ashes of humiliating defeat. It was this group which built the foundations of what eventually became the Sony Corporation.

The official history of Sony likes to make much of the company's humble, under-funded and undercapitalised beginnings, in a cramped corner of a Tokyo department store. However, the facts do not fit the romantic story told by Akio Morita, a story parroted down the years by Sony's public relations machine. In war-torn Japan, premises were difficult to obtain for business. Electrical power, for instance, was by no means universal, even in Tokyo, and fuel to run generators had to be imported. Morita could not possibly have obtained the facilities that came his way without extremely good connections, particularly with the American occupation forces. The under-funding and under-capitalisation can be accounted for easily. Very little capital was available anywhere, savings had been decimated, and what money could be accessed was in dollars provided by the Americans or in yen, which at the time were worthless outside Japan and not very well regarded inside the country. Conventional economics simply did not apply in post-war Japan.

Akio Morita, however, came from a long-established family, whose four hundred year-old brewery business was one of the country's major manufacturers of the national drink, Sake. Before war intervened, Morita was being groomed so that eventually he would take over and run the operation. His connections were impeccable. With his family background it should come as no surprise that, once the occupying powers accepted that his enthusiasm for their priorities was genuine, Morita managed to secure essential government contracts and loan guarantees. Meanwhile, the Japanese people, after the deprivations of three years of an intense war, were avaricious for cheap consumer goods. Totsuko enjoyed two other major advantages: it employed some of the best scientists and engineers in Japan and it could operate as a near-monopoly. The authorities decided who was acceptable and few could match Morita in that regard. In addition, Totsuko was far ahead of most other electronics suppliers in that its key personnel brought knowledge of their secret wartime experiments to the company. Far from a struggle against the odds, success was almost guaranteed from the outset.

Only the complete collapse of the economy could cause Totsuko's failure. Since the new Japanese constitution and economic system were created by the Americans, who backed their enterprise with a ready supply of dollars, that was unlikely to happen. The US would not allow it. The Americans were also concerned to ensure that the aggrandising and militaristic tendencies of imperial Japan did not reappear. This was a fine line to walk as they allowed Emperor Hirohito to remain Head of State and did not carry out a wholesale purge of the existing Japanese bureaucracy. It was therefore important to the US that those they considered important to this end were gainfully employed in the furtherance of the new Japan (this was a variation of the policy of de-nazification the US carried out in Germany. In that case, many of the German scientists and engineers who worked for Hitler found their way onto the US space, nuclear weapons and ballistic missile programmes).

After the war, Morita conveyed the impression that he underwent an almost Pauline conversion when hostilities were approaching their horrific conclusion in 1945. His Road to Damascus was all around him. Everywhere he went he was surrounded by the devastation that only war or catastrophic natural disaster can bring. Thus he became convinced that he and his team of experts should dedicate their talents to help achieve a Japan that honoured its culture while eschewing its historic military aggression and quest for empire. The new Japan should embrace the world economic system and create a country that could stand proud in the world once again. This time it would not be through war but by putting two characteristics Morita saw as defining the Japanese identity – technological innovation and hard work – to a peaceful and economically successful objective.

Amazingly, this was exactly what the Americans had in mind for post-war Japan. A dynamic economy was to be created, under which the population exchanged imperial pretensions (and thus a possible insurrection) for employment security and the consumer society. It was the MacArthur-inspired US prescription for its former enemy. This would cost money but the US had that in abundance and was prepared to spend it. When Morita converted to the new religion, he was welcomed by the Americans with open arms.

Once Totsuko was up and running it was supported by the arcane Japanese banking industry (Sony later founded its own bank) and signed agreements with government to supply volt-meters, which were necessary to repair Japan's destroyed electricity infrastructure. These two deals alone guaranteed the fledgling company both cash flow and profits. Just as important, they gave Morita and his team the means to devote time and money to an endeavour closer to their hearts, namely, research at the cutting edge of the impending global technological revolution, a revolution which would be inspired and led from Japan, after being stolen from the United States.

There was another feature of Akio Morita's new enterprise, one that would have far-reaching effects on Japanese society. In the scheme of things it is even more important than the incredible technological innovations which have been the hallmark of Sony down the years. Morita realised it was not enough to aspire to material improvement. The Japanese yearning for honour had been badly dented by the Second World War. So poisonous has this legacy been that the Japanese people are in denial to this day about the behaviour of their military forces (comprised of ordinary conscripts) during the conflict. Sixty years after the war came to an end, textbooks in Japanese schools continue to gloss over the worst aspects of the way they conducted their wartime operations.

Morita recognised that culturally, Japan had taken what originally might have been a noble ideal – honour – and given it a value so high that it became an essential ingredient of Japanese self-identity. Unfortunately, it was a small step from there to belief in racial and cultural superiority. Morita also saw that the manipulation of the ideal had led Japan to disaster. His insight was profound. It was both undesirable and probably impossible, he understood, to rid the nation of values imbued over centuries, no matter how corrupted they had become. But neither could the issue be ignored. What was required was a re-direction of this national characteristic.

As Totsuko progressed, it began to gain a public profile. One day, a member of PIRC who had not remained a part of Morita's group after the war saw a newspaper article about Morita and his new company. Or some reports have it that it was the other way round, with Morita reading an article about a PIRC engineer. Whatever, Morita contacted his old colleague and a relationship was renewed that was to last decades and in the process alter the lifestyle of billions of people all over the world. His name was Masaru Ibuka. Ibuka and Morita came up with a corporate philosophy which transferred the allegiance of the Japanese worker from old and discredited institutions to the new corporations. These companies would be the saviours of Japan and the redeemers of its national pride. Every area of a worker's life was to be designed around the notion that employees should subsume individuality for the corporate good. The company should supply all the necessary elements of life, from housing to the ritual of singing the company song, freeing the people to concentrate on improving their productivity. In return, workers would have a job for life. Many years later, Ibuka was behind Sony's formation of an educational foundation which promulgated this philosophy. The foundation also published Ibuka's thoughts on child-rearing.

Morita and Ibuka created the Japanese model, copied not only in Japan itself but eventually, after first indifference, then dismissal, all around the globe. By that time, however, the Japanese had already changed the world. The essence of the Morita-Ibuka idea can be seen in the original mission-statement, issued in 1947. It is all there. The document, officially called the Founding Prospectus, sets out what Morita and Ibuka hoped to achieve. It says that 'not just anyone' could join the new enterprise, 'but those with similar resolve' (to themselves). The company was comprised of people who had 'naturally come together to embark on this new mission with the rebirth of Japan after the war.' The aim was 'to create a stable work environment where engineers ... could realise their societal mission'. Under a section entitled: 'Purposes of incorporation', clause B sums it up precisely. The corporation was formed, it says, 'To reconstruct Japan and to elevate the nation's culture through dynamic technological and manufacturing activities'. It appears to me that the philosophy was designed to deflect guilt over wartime behaviour, which might have led to difficult questions about the nature of what it means to be Japanese. It goes on to put forward a vision of a new, democratic and economically successful Japan. Corporations and those that worked for them were presented as the hope for the future, a force for public good, embodying the true nature of the nation and its culture. Stripped of its pseudo-religious connotations, the state was destined to become more technocratic. Emperor Hirohito was no longer a god but he wasn't quite a man either. Stability, economic growth and loyalty to the company were the new commandments. It was music to the Americans' ears.

After the Americans and the Japanese government gave Morita and Ibuka their head, the new corporation went from strength to strength. The achievements of the researchers, designers, technologists and marketers cannot be underestimated. The real innovation to put Sony on the map was the world's first small-sized – 'pocketable', as Sony described it – transistor radio, the revolutionary TR-63, introduced in 1957 to an astonished world. However, the way Sony obtained the original plans for production of the radio was somewhat underhand. When Masaru Ibuka heard that the Bell Corporation in the USA had managed to produce a working transistor, he refused to believe it had a future. He had made his own primitive versions during and since the war and was convinced that certain technical problems could not be overcome sufficiently to allow commercial production. He was soon proved wrong.

When the General Electric Company began production of transistors, mainly for the US military, Akio Morita took action to rectify Ibuka's mistake. He dispatched one of his most trusted engineers, Kazuo Iwama, to visit the General Electric factory in America to find out what he could about the production line. Iwama was welcomed with open arms as an emissary from the US forces in Japan, recommended by General MacArthur himself in the interests of post-war Japanese-American cooperation. That did not extend, however, as far as supplying Iwama with blueprints of the General Electric production line. General Electric did give him the run of the factory, though, and let him talk to whomever he chose. Each night, when he returned to his hotel room, he would immediately make notes and drawings of everything he had seen. These were sent back to Tokyo, where they became known as the Iwama Reports.

The motive behind Morita's plan to steal as much as possible from the US company was that Sony needed to use US production knowledge in its own technology. Morita had briefed Iwama to find out as much as he could clandestinely. Otherwise, why would Iwama play the cloak-and-dagger act instead of making his notes and drawings while he was in the factory, where they would have been far more accurate than those made from memory some hours later? That Iwama's drawings could not be used as a blueprint, thereby ensuring Sony had to develop its own machine tools, does not detract from the fact that Iwama provided much valuable information. The Iwama Reports solved some of Sony's basic technical questions in the production of small transistor radios and saved several years of possible cul-de-sacs. It was wartime technology allied to the post-war knowledge-economy that gave the world its first taste of what the Japanese could do.

To be fair to the expertise of the PIRC/Sony engineers, their contribution to the TR-63 and thereafter was immense. There were tape recorders and a new and better magnetic tape, the revolutionary Trinitron television, the sensational Walkman, the first CD player in 1982, the Camcorder in 1985. At every turn there was innovation, expert design and brilliant marketing. Well, at almost every turn. There were the Betamax and the MiniDisc debacles but despite these, Sony's rise to global dominance was inexorable.

Two years after the TR-63 shook the world, a 29 year-old graduate of the Berlin University of Arts became an unlikely employee of the Sony Corporation. His name was Norio Ohga, a Japanese musician and conductor of considerable talent who had been offered his place in Berlin following a mercurial three years studying at the Tokyo National University of Fine Arts and Music, from which he graduated in 1953. Throughout his student years, Ohga supplemented his income through being regularly consulted by Sony over the quality of its products, particularly those intended for musical reproduction or broadcasting purposes. When the chance came to work for the corporation full-time in 1959, Ohga eschewed the possibility of a career in the concert halls of the world in favour of making his contribution to Morita's new Japan.

Such was Ohga's impact at Sony that by 1964 he was a director and Manager of the Product Planning Division. He was the natural choice to head the joint venture record company with CBS in 1968. Ohga benefited directly and personally a number of times over the years from Sony's involvement with CBS. In the 1968 Sony/CBS company, which distributed CBS records throughout Japan, Ohga was the Senior Managing Director. Coming from his musical background, it should be no surprise that as he rose through the ranks of the corporation, Ohga developed a vision beyond the invention and sale of hardware. Traditional Sony strengths would always lead to innovative electronic devices but for Norio Ohga, a new future for the corporation he adored beckoned. Entertainment! In a word, software.

After his elevation in 1968, Ohga was unstoppable. By 1972 he was Managing Director of the Sony Corporation and by 1974, Senior Managing Director. It is difficult actually to discern exactly when the torch is passed in Japanese corporations. Unlike European or American companies, one regime is not generally replaced in one move. The old guard gradually steps aside, occupying a series of posts with titles like Chairman of the Board. In fact, the process is designed to retain honour, leaving without being seen to have left, a revered elder statesman. Somewhere in the mid-seventies, this fate befell the now-aging Akio Morita. As the spy, Kazuo Iwama, assumed the supreme office, Ohga rose to President and Chief Operating Officer in 1982, then to President and Chief Executive Officer in 1989. That promotion came at Ohga's zenith, just after the acquisitions of CBS Records and Columbia Pictures. According to sources at the old CBS, including Walter Yetnikoff, Ohga also made a packet of personal wealth from the takeovers.

Norio Ohga was also the scourge of George Michael. Paul Russell was Sony's major witness in the law-suit that Michael brought against the company in the high court in London in the mid 1990s. Russell explained how he answered a phone call late on a Friday from one of Sony's lawyers. 'I've received a letter from George Michael's solicitor,' Russell was told. 'Michael wants to get out of his recording contract with Sony Music'. Michael evidently believed the label was not promoting him in a way commensurate with his own view of his artistic merits. On one of those spring afternoons in 2005 on the lawn of Russell's house in Wentworth, he told me the story. The important part is the meeting Paul arranged in New York between Norio Ohga and George Michael in November 1995. At the meeting, Michael was due to give an impassioned plea to be released from his contract with Sony otherwise he would go to court. Paul Russell said that he told Michael's advisors that when the Pink Floyd's guitarist, Roger Waters, wanted to get out of his own contract, Russell gave him a little speech to make to Norio Ohga, stressing the money they all had made in the previous few years and that now the time had come for the parting of the ways. It worked. Waters was released from his contract. However, at the time, Waters was not flavour of the month and his records were not selling well. George Michael was a different story.

Ohga listened politely to George Michael's case then suddenly, without warning, stopped Michael in his tracks by producing one of Sony's new mini-digital cameras and taking Michael's picture while the singer was in full flow. Ohga then abruptly left the room. He was not prepared to countenance Michael's pleas, which he saw as without basis and a slur on Sony's reputation. Translated, that meant that Sony was not about to relinquish one of its major earners. They would pay George Michael more money but they would not let him go.

There was no room for compromise. George Michael carried on with his ill-advised litigation. Sony won the case with ease. Soon afterwards, the American record mogul, David Geffen, met with the Sony board in London and bought out Michael's recording contract. 'How much will it cost to release George?', Geffen asked. 'A hell of a lot of money', was the reply. 'Is this enough?', Geffen said, producing a cheque for $30 million. Remember, in the 1980s and 90s, Michael was one of the world's best selling artists. 'Yes, yes, yes,' was the response. Geffen bailed Sony out because although the company won the court case and therefore George Michael was still under contract, the singer refused to produce further music. Moreover, Sony felt they couldn't enforce the ruling that they could recover their legal costs from the artist. That would make matters worse. The impasse remained until David Geffen's intervention. Within five years, however, George Michael was once again a Sony artist. Do not bet against the same thing happening with Michael Jackson.

It was no wonder Norio Ohga was in no mood to succumb to George Michael's blandishments. One year earlier, he was the man in charge when the Jordan Chandler scandal broke around Michael Jackson's head. Ohga was horrified. It was less than three years since he and Akio Morita had authorised a possible fifteen-year commitment to Jackson. At the time it seemed a no-brainer. The most popular artist in music history had agreed to re-sign, there was to be a guaranteed flow of albums and any number of other opportunities, including movies. Now, not only was all that in jeopardy, but Sony's carefully cultivated image of a family-friendly company and its core strategy of diversification was under threat from the Jackson revelations.

Ohga was desperate to keep his organisation at as great a distance as possible from the star. But Sony still had to release and market Jackson's records. This balancing act was not easy since it meant throwing the whole of the company's marketing strategy suddenly into reverse. Nonetheless, it had to be done. Ohga would have preferred to rid his company of Jackson there and then but that was not possible.

It is quite incredible and a testament to Ohga and his mentor, Morita, that through both the Chandler scandal of 1993–4 and Jackson's arrest and trial of 2003–5, Sony was rarely mentioned in the same breath as the star. Sony had made huge amounts of cash from Michael Jackson and the company had connived in promoting the singer's bizarre image. Surely they had a duty of care to their artist, didn't they? When Martin Bashir was forced into the Santa Maria court to testify in 2005, he was accompanied by a bevy of lawyers, provided and paid for by ABC. My investigations have failed to turn up one example of a similar show of support from Sony for Michael Jackson, either in 1994, when no criminal offence was prosecuted, or in the Arvizo case ten years later. Nor, for that matter, at any time in between.

When the Chandler allegations were made public in 1993, Ohga spoke to Akio Morita, who by then was a figurehead with no direct responsibilities or job. He was, in effect, retired, although he still held the position of Chairman of the Board. He had been, however, Ohga's close partner in the acquisition of CBS. Between them, they decided that the main thing to do was to say nothing unless forced to do so. Everything connected to Michael Jackson was delegated down the chain of command to A&R and marketing departments in Sony's local offices around the world. Their job was to keep things quiet until the outcome of the Chandler business was determined. If there was any co-ordination at all it would be provided by the international record division in New York or by the American label, also in New York and now run by Tommy Mottola. As for the Sony Corporation generally, especially in Japan, Jackson came to resemble one of those Soviet politburo members, who, when removed from power, was also erased from all photographs as if he had never existed. Sony had also been using Michael Jackson to further its corporate aims. At Jackson gigs Sony provided tickets and hospitality for many hundreds in each concert location. The takeover of CBS had been finalised at a Michael Jackson show in Tokyo, attended by Norio Ohga and a retinue of Sony and CBS executives. All of that was now over. From 1994 Jackson occupied a sort of no-man's land at Sony somewhere between grudging acceptance and outright denial.

The executives at Sony were mightily relieved when Jackson settled the Chandler matter and averted a criminal trial. It was not the perfect solution but it limited the damage to the company. Norio Ohga could not possibly leave it there, however, that would be a dereliction of duty. What if it happened again? Ohga saw his task as ensuring Sony kept its distance from Jackson but continued to recoup on its investment. It would still be possible to make ever larger profits from the singer if everything went well. Ohga decided on a long game. Jackson would be monitored. In the meantime, Sony would fulfil its contractual obligations but do no more than was absolutely necessary. So when 'Invincible' was allocated a marketing budget of $25 million, who could argue that Sony was not behind Jackson. But there is a huge difference between spending money and spending it effectively. Many would say that in most territories the cash was, in large measure, wasted.

What Sony wanted at the end of it all was ownership of Jackson's back catalogue, including 'Thriller'. Ohga and Morita were also in the process of negotiating a deal with Jackson's lawyers to acquire half of Jackson's ATV music publishing interests. Morita was determined to push this deal through no matter what. He certainly did not let his moral outrage extend to pulling out of a lucrative money-spinner. But total control was on his mind. That would mean getting Jackson out of the Sony ATV music publishing company altogether at some point. To achieve this it would be necessary eventually, to destroy Jackson's career.

Meanwhile, to divert attention from its association with the world's most famous alleged paedophile, Sony embarked on a corporate reorganisation. Since the days of Ibuka and Morita, Sony's structure had actually been modelled on the wartime PIRC operation, with superficially autonomous units coming under a centralised command. Scientists and engineers drove policy, while objectives were handed down through a rigid hierarchy. Ohga, however, would not profit from the reorganisation. In fact, he had brought dishonour on Sony despite managing to limit the damage Jackson had caused. The problems with Michael Jackson were seen as a direct result of Ohga's strategic decision to turn Sony into a global entertainment corporation.

Ohga was not retired, exactly. The Japanese don't do things like that. And anyway, it was Ohga's task to ensure Sony extricated itself from Michael Jackson. But when you study the minutiae of Japanese corporate titles, you can sometimes read the runes. From President and CEO, positions he had held since 1989, Ohga became Chairman and CEO, a subtle but tangible signal that his days at the helm were numbered. The new President was Nobuyuki Idei, not a mystical artist like Ohga but a hard nosed marketer with a thorough knowledge of electronics. Idei became joint CEO with Ohga in 1998. Norio Ohga was then Chairman and joint CEO.

After his success in seeing off the threat posed by George Michael and his belief that he had contained the Jackson-Chandler fallout, Ohga was confident his next move would be decisive. He completed the purchase of half of ATV Music, which was renamed Sony ATV. In 1999, he oversaw the huge borrowings Michael Jackson took out with the Bank of America using his stock in Sony ATV as collateral. Indeed Ohga encouraged it. If Jackson defaulted, the Bank of America would own his shares and as far as Ohga was concerned the bank was a much more reliable partner for Sony than the wayward pop star. Ohga knew the initial loan would not be enough and that Jackson would be back for more. At virtually the same moment, Akio Morita drew his last breath. It was now all up to Norio Ohga to preserve Sony's honour. After Morita's death, Ohga's title was changed once more. He was no longer joint CEO. He now held the ominous post of Chairman of the Board.

Michael Jackson did indeed need more... and more. Then came *Living with Michael Jackson*. It was time to pass some information to the Santa Barbara District Attorney's office. Tom Sneddon's case was, at this stage, either incomplete or essentially deficient, depending on who you believe. He had no evidence of abuse prior to the broadcast of Martin Bashir's programme. How could he make abuse charges stick which were supposed to have occurred after the screening of the programme, when the public uproar was at its peak? He desperately needed something else, something which would lock all the pieces together.

The information concerning Jackson's finances, which neither Sneddon nor anyone else could have guessed, gave the prosecutor exactly what he required. Michael Jackson's career was in the doldrums, Sony could give proof of that. His borrowings were such that if the investigations proceeded to a trial, it could well bankrupt the singer as he would be forced to default on his loans. To Sneddon, that knowledge was crucial.

Sneddon now had a narrative he thought he could credibly present to a jury. It went something like this: Jackson needed his career to return to its previous heights, not just to feed his ego but because he would otherwise go broke in a big and very public way. That was why he decided to let Martin Bashir into his life. The television show would provide a platform from which Jackson could stave off the creditors and kick-start a new and even more successful period in his career. It was to be the final step in Jackson's rehabilitation, almost ten years after the Chandler affair shattered his reputation. When it all went wrong, the singer must have known that if he couldn't salvage the situation, everything he had worked for would be taken away. It would be an unbearable humiliation.

This is where the conspiracy charge comes into play. As Sneddon described it, Jackson's finances were in such a parlous state he would do anything to save himself. That was the motive for the detention of the Arvizos and the insistence they deny everything on tape in a rebuttal video, which Jackson thought would save him. Jackson could not do all that himself but since he had a huge payroll there were plenty willing to do his bidding. In other words, this was how and why the conspiracy occurred. Part of these desperate measures included attempts by Jackson to further ingratiate himself with Gavin Arvizo, to the extent that he plied the boy with alcohol and committed the lewd acts with which he was later charged.

This, at any rate, was Tom Sneddon's version of events now he had the financial information. It provided motive for the conspiracy and the abuse. The conspiracy was pivotal to his case. There have been many commentators and legal experts who could not explain why Sneddon went with the conspiracy charge. But to Sneddon, it was the central act in his drama. Technically, he was entitled, if he really believed his account, to bring the charge. But in reality he was so driven in his quest he became blind to the absurdity of his argument.

The source of the leak was carefully concealed. If my information is correct, even from the Santa Barbara DA. I have been told that the story emanated from Tokyo but was delivered from New York. Something 'very, very devilish' had indeed been going on. It is unsurprising that Sony's lawyers were so concerned Paul Russell had put two and two together they tried to intimidate him into silence.

5

DUNKIRK

At this point, I should declare an interest. I am a party to a contract with Sony. Like Michael Jackson's, it was a contract picked up by Sony when the company took over CBS. Also like Michael Jackson, the terms were subsequently renegotiated, although the numbers in my case would be loose change in the Jackson contract. In the original summer of love, 1967, I was a sixteen-year old who had a passion for playing music. After attending an audition along with a number of other young hopefuls I got the job and joined a band called The Love Affair as a keyboard player. After a few months playing the club circuit around Great Britain we came up with a record that was destined to be a classic down the years. You might know the song: 'Everlasting Love'. The record label was CBS.

While CBS was a household name in the USA in the 1960s, it was not such a force outside North America, especially since its television network was for domestic consumption only. As far as its record labels were concerned, CBS's huge roster of major artists sold in large quantities all over the world but they were licenced to local companies in each region from CBS's International division in New York. This began to change when CBS Records opened up its first oversees operation, in the UK, where it had maintained a bureau supplying stories to CBS television news in the USA for many years. The company's head office and creative division were located in London, on Theobalds Road in Holborn, with the record pressing plant and distribution centre in Aylesbury, a small town about an hour north of the capital.

The UK company's profits were built on records which originated in America. The supreme quality of the American artists – luminaries such as Barbra Streisand, Simon and Garfunkel and Bob Dylan – as well as their sheer number, ensured CBS's success. In Britain, the label was given the name CBS, unlike the USA, where the company owned two labels,

Columbia and Epic. This was because in the USA, by the time the record division was founded, CBS was already an established brand through its long tradition of radio and television broadcasts. In addition, the main CBS board were always uneasy about the record business. They loved the money the record division brought (it helped subsidise the huge cost of quality news-gathering) but they always thought that some artist or executive might embarrass them and threaten their television licence. So, although everyone knew CBS owned the labels, they were given separate names. In Europe, where CBS had no broadcasting interests, the record label could also be used to promote brand awareness of the corporation itself, hence the use of the parent company's name for the UK label.

CBS UK soon began to come under pressure from the New York headquarters, in the person of the CEO and general overlord, Clive Davis, to find bands and produce some hits locally. This was because the American charts had been swamped in the 1960s by British artists, the so-called 'British Invasion' led by the Beatles (whose records were released on EMI's Parlaphone label in the UK), the Rolling Stones (on Decca) and the Kinks (on Pye). The Love Affair was one of CBS's first signings of a non-American band and 'Everlasting Love' was the result. The record was released in the UK in November 1967, entered the British charts in December and hit number one at the beginning of January 1968. It subsequently reached number one in fourteen countries and was a top ten hit in another ten. It provided CBS UK with the perfect repost to Clive Davis' urgings.

'Everlasting Love' kicked off a run of chart success for the UK company that lasted until Sony bought CBS in 1988 and beyond. After Paul Russell took over in the seventies, the performance of the London operation reached outrageous levels. David Essex, Jeff Wayne, Sade and the biggest of them all, Abba, are just a handful of the amazing series of international hits coming out of London. In the case of Abba, CBS owned the rights for the UK only. This was because Paul Russell developed a strong personal relationship with Abba's eccentric producer and manager, Stig Anderson. Russell had been enthusiastic about the band before they had released a record. After Abba's huge success, Russell and Anderson would meet each November in Sweden to negotiate a deal for the new album. Stig would only agree one album at a time but he continued to operate in this manner for years with people and labels he liked. The two would begin their discussions with a drinking binge. Of course, the talks went on all night and required lots of listening to loud music. With sometimes only an hour left to catch his plane back to London, Russell, after three days and nights of Anderson's hospitality, finalised the deal, which he wrote on a spare piece of scrap paper. Russell would then telephone the CBS factory in Aylesbury and authorise the immediate pressing of Abba's new LP.

Stig Anderson didn't think much of CBS executives in other territories, particularly the USA. He preferred to make country-by-country deals with people he liked. It also enabled him to keep control of the whole Abba project. This caused some resentment of the London CBS operation by those in charge of CBS companies elsewhere. Some of them felt that Paul Russell was not pressing Stig enough to get a world-wide deal. The truth was, Stig just didn't want Abba on CBS anywhere except the UK and that was the end of it.

At one time in the 1980s, CBS virtually took over the top five best-selling records in Britain for a period of about two years. This run brought the attentions of the press, who, convinced there must be payola (unlawful payment for radio airplay) going on, dispatched undercover reporters to find the story. They followed Paul Russell and Managing Director, Maurice Oberstein. The intrepid men from the newspapers even went through CBS's garbage. However, the journalists were unable to uncover any evidence whatever to support their contention and the investigations soon ceased. Years later, after CBS became Sony, payola was alleged and admitted in the USA after an investigation in New York State.

As the London branch was so successful, the main CBS board in New York embarked upon a huge international expansion programme. It was aggressive, to say the least. It worked like this. CBS would approach a reasonably successful local record label in a given territory, say New Zealand. They would offer the local company a licence for the exclusive rights in the territory to release CBS records originating in America. These were some of the best selling artists in the world. CBS would often inject some marketing cash in exchange for a minority shareholding. When the licence period was due to expire, normally after about three years, and the local company had become dependent on the CBS product, even going into debt to expand, CBS would inform them that the licence would not be renewed unless CBS took a controlling stake in the company. The shareholders in the local company were now over a barrel. Most took the money. It wasn't long before CBS was in total control and the original owners were history.

As for myself, after a couple more hits with The Love Affair and a contribution to the band's first LP, I decamped to the Robert Stigwood Organisation. Stigwood, perhaps the greatest manager in the history of popular music, with credits to his name such as The Bee Gees, Eric Clapton, 'Saturday Night Fever' and 'Grease', looked after my interests for the next five years.

Four of the five members of The Love Affair, including me, were minors, therefore CBS was legally obliged to ensure that a proper contract for our services existed. Thus unlike many hit artists of the period, my royalties were protected. While I was in the Love Affair a young guy about my age named John McIndoe, who was an aspiring singer and actor, came to see us playing a gig in Blackpool. We became friends and remain so to this day. Eighteen months after we first met, John attended an audition in London, where two Hollywood producers, Sid and Marty Croft, were casting for a new US television show. John got the part and was whisked to Los Angeles where he became one of the stars of the hit TV show *The Bugaloos*. Although he made money from the show, his royalties were not entirely protected and in subsequent years, when the show and its music enjoyed a revival, John did not receive the amounts he believed were his due.

The royalty rate paid to the Love Affair in the 1960s – a miserly 2% – would be laughed at today. When Michael Jackson was signed to Motown as one member of the Jackson 5, their combined royalty rate was 2½%. As the years rolled by the invention of new formats like cassettes and compact discs, as well as the advent of oldies radio stations and an increasingly insatiable appetite for sixties music, meant that Love Affair records, particularly 'Everlasting Love', began to sell all over again. Moreover, the quantities were larger than they had ever been, even in our heyday. When McDonalds and Coca-Cola wanted to use our recording in a television advertising campaign, Sony, who had taken over CBS a decade earlier, agreed to renegotiate our contract.

The negotiations took a number of years to complete and the legal fees were exorbitant but eventually Sony agreed an upgrade in royalties amounting to some 800%, backdated to 1967. Forensic accounting showed that both CBS and Sony had underpaid us in the preceding years, even though the rate was a paltry 2%. This was taken care of with a cash adjustment. A sort of second peak was reached in 2004, when the Love Affair's 'Everlasting Love' was used prominently in the movie, *Bridget Jones: The Edge of Reason* starring Rene Zellweger, Hugh Grant and Colin Firth.

I don't think my association with Sony has clouded my judgment in the matter of Michael Jackson. It is coincidental that I happen to have a contract with the same record company as the King of Pop but my dealings with Sony have been in the form of a normal commercial arrangement, without the mayhem that has always attended the affairs of Michael Jackson. However, it does mean that when I write about Sony I have some personal experience of how the company works and I know people from within the corporation, both now and in the past, who have an intimate knowledge of its secrets.

Following Michael Jackson's settlement with Jordan Chandler, Norio Ohga and Akio Morita decided that it was injudicious for Sony to continue to associate itself with the singer. The greatest area of exposure, yet, ironically, the biggest opportunity, concerned ownership of Sony ATV. Sony wanted it desperately but running a company with a suspected paedophile was not the kind of image Sony wanted to project. But the corporation did not wish to forgo its own share, which would have been the simplest course of action. This was because it was becoming clear that the $50 million Sony was about to pay Michael Jackson for 50% of the company was a snip. The resultant Sony ATV company was seriously undervalued and the reason for that was the incredible ongoing earning power of the songs of John Lennon and Paul McCartney. When Jackson bought ATV Music Publishing it was worth $47 million. By the time Sony took its half-share, the value had doubled. Because music publishing produces a constant revenue-stream, and in the case of Sony ATV, an ever-increasing flow of cash, Sony's accountants reckoned the publishing company was worth at least $250 million and that figure could only go higher. In fact, in my opinion, the company was worth twice that even then and I believe it to be still undervalued. I reckon its 2006 worth is at least $1.5 billion and rising, with an annual income of $200 million, nearly all of it profit. Ohga and Morita were not about to give that up.

Walter Yetnikoff was, through the 1970s and 80s, the wunderkind of the record industry, an über-executive if ever there was one. And he worked for CBS. Yetnikoff was notorious in the music business for his outrageous behaviour, foul-mouthed language and prodigious use of alcohol and drugs, particularly cocaine, which he referred to as 'milk'. He was also extremely adept at finding talented artists and keeping them happy. This meant he was given much latitude within the CBS Corporation, particularly by his early mentor in the company, Clive Davis. However, despite his infamy in the record business and his self-styled title, King of Records, he was virtually unknown in the real world.

He put this to rights with his autobiography, *Howling at the Moon*, published in 2003. In it, Yetnikoff manages to convey the mad world of rock-and-roll in the CBS years only too well. 'The great paradox that sat at the centre of my life,' he writes, 'was that the more I misbehaved, the more the company profited. Profits were my tickets to entitlement, craziness my reward. I could have anything. The more records we sold, the less the corporation understood how we did it, the more absolute my autonomy. The insane profitability of my professional life allowed me to lead a personal life, equally insane, free of reason or restraint.' It was not a state of affairs liable to be tolerated for too long by the corporate raiders from Tokyo.

In the first chapter of his book, Yetnikoff tells an anecdote about Michael Jackson. One day Yetnikoff received a telephone call from Jackson, who had an urgent request. Apparently, the record and film mogul, David Geffen, had asked Jackson if one of the singer's recordings could be used in a forthcoming movie Geffen was producing, *Days of Thunder*, starring Tom Cruise. Jackson said 'yes'. But, he told Yetnikoff, he didn't actually want his song in the picture. He therefore asked Yetnikoff, in his role as CBS executive and thus owner of the recording's copyright, to say 'no' to Geffen. More than that, Jackson wanted Yetnikoff to take the blame for the rejection by telling Geffen he was overruling the singer. This, according to Yetnikoff, he did.

To the best of my knowledge, Michael Jackson has neither verified nor denied the story and David Geffen has refrained from commenting on the affair. So we only have the ambiguous and unreliable word of Yetnikoff. Essentially, *Howling at the Moon* can be divided into two areas. First, is the glib, unconcerned-about-anything-or-anyone Yetnikoff, the persona at the centre of the above tale. Second is the born-again Yetnikoff of today, confessing his numerous sins, fearlessly telling the truth and a seeker after redemption. I asked someone who has known Yetnikoff for many years about the veracity or otherwise of his account. 'I would say it's pretty much accurate,' he replied. Then my source remembered a conversation with Yetnikoff in 2003, not long after the publication of *Howling at the Moon*. 'I saw Walter at the time, before I'd read his book. I said to him: "I hear you've got a book coming out". He said, "Well, it was a book but then the lawyers got hold of it and now it's a pamphlet."'

The point of this story is as follows. It is the job of a record company or music publisher to maximise income from recordings and songs under their control. This is especially true for public companies quoted on a stock exchange, which are compelled to give priority to the share price and the bottom line. There can be no doubt that when the chance comes along for a recording to be used in a Tom Cruise/David Geffen vehicle, you take it with both hands. If one person can say 'no' on what turns out to be a whim, then any corporation would be extremely concerned. Into the future, anything could happen. Since Michael Jackson had done this very thing, he was bound to be perceived, sooner or later, as a loose cannon. And if someone with the reputation of a Walter Yetnikoff is around, such a person would have to be very loose indeed to wrest away that soubriquet.

The blue pencils of the attorneys notwithstanding, there are a couple of other tantalising glimpses into the world of the music business in Yetnikoff's tome. Years before Sony bought CBS, the two companies entered into a joint venture record company in Japan, which had proved remarkably successful. However, Sony refused to pay the required dividends to CBS. Norio Ohga and Akio Morita claimed that under Japanese law, their corporation was barred from paying such dividends to an overseas company even when that company owned a significant block of shares. According to Yetnikoff, a group of CBS executives, including him, was sent to Tokyo to sort the matter out. Ohga and Morita refused to budge and the Americans left empty handed. But before he left, Yetnikoff says that Ohga sought him out and apologised. 'I'll find a way of making it up to you,' Ohga told Yetnikoff, before adding, 'In future we'll do big business together.' The clear implication is that Ohga had already decided on the long-term pursuit of CBS and was using the ability to withhold dividends as a part of his strategy. Akio Morita, who was still nominally head of Sony, went a stage further. 'We are determined,' he said, 'We are patient'.

What Ohga had seen was that in the 1980s, CBS had become vulnerable to a takeover. It was the era of rampant capitalism and corporate takeovers were becoming the norm. CBS was slow to recognise the importance of the Ted Turner revolution, which created CNN and made cable viable. Ted Turner started his meteoric rise with a small, local television station in Atlanta, Georgia. Turner renamed his operation a super-station, delivering lowest common denominator entertainment programmes throughout the USA via satellite and cable. He was interviewed by BBC Television's Peter Snow, who asked Turner in typical BBC fashion, 'What would you do if America's traditional networks like CBS stopped doing news and just broadcast cheap entertainment like you?' 'I'd do news, you dummy,' was Turner's reply. It was not long before Turner, true to his word, devised the concept of 24-hour rolling news – CNN.

Moreover, the CBS television operation had lost its long-held position as the number one television network in the US. As CBS's legendary leader, Bill Paley, told Walter Yetnikoff, 'It's going to get worse before it gets better. The vultures … they smell blood, they're circling the sky. The vultures are about to descend.' It would not be the last time that word – vultures – would crop up in this story.

William S. Paley had been in charge of CBS for over forty years. By the 1980s, he seemed to lose the will to fight and after a frenzied share-buying spree by Larry Tisch, who controlled the Loews Corporation (and owned Tiffany's at the same time), Paley, the man who had set the standard in US radio and television, was more or less gone. Tisch wanted to offload the record division and consolidate CBS's television interests. Although there were several potential suitors, it was the Sony Corporation which ended up paying almost $2 billion to acquire CBS Records. It was not an easy pursuit. Many wheels had to be oiled and more than once the deal looked dead in the water. Early on in the proceedings, for instance, Norio Ohga suffered a heart attack while watching a performance of the Mozart Opera, *Don Giovanni*. It appeared heart problems were a fact of life for Ohga. This time he told Walter Yetnikoff that he'd 'be fine if you get CBS to accept our offer.' It was Yetnikoff who told Morita that the man to deal with at CBS was no longer Bill Paley, it was Larry Tisch.

Tisch, however, was procrastinating. The Sony offer had gone from $1.25 billion to $2 billion and no doubt Tisch thought he could get even more out of the Japanese. Then came the stock market crash of 1987 and, as Yetnikoff noticed, 'The $2 billion offer suddenly looked good.' Within a month, Tisch, Paley and the CBS board accepted the Sony offer. Before long, the New York Times ran a photo featuring Cyndi Lauper giving Akio Morita a hug. 'The Americans,' observed Morita, 'have lost their edge'.

A year before the takeover, Walter Yetnikoff appointed Tommy Mottola to a senior position in the American record label. After Sony's acquisition,

Yetnikoff encouraged Morita and Ohga to buy a major movie studio. Eventually, Sony bought Columbia Pictures but Yetnikoff was left out of the loop as he was in rehab for his various drink and drug problems when the purchase went through.

In 1990, Norio Ohga began to shift his allegiance away from Walter Yetnikoff. Yetnikoff had worked with Ohga either in the joint venture record company or the new Sony Music Entertainment enterprise for twenty-five years. In addition, Yetnikoff had helped facilitate Sony's purchase of CBS and in the process made the Japanese vast amounts of cash – the US record division made over $400 million profit in 1989 alone. But Yetnikoff was beginning to lose the trust of some of the record label's major artists, including Billy Joel, Bruce Springsteen and, most importantly, Michael Jackson. There can be no doubt that of all the Sony executives involved, Tommy Mottola was instrumental in the demise of Yetnikoff, whispering poisonous stories into the ears of the artists and their managers. Yetnikoff's outrageous attitude and behaviour, the very traits that had endeared him both to his employers and the rock stars he signed to CBS down the years, had finally caught up with him, ironically, just as he was giving up excess and taking up God.

In the music business, all kinds of madness are tolerated, even encouraged. In my day, if you failed to consume the requisite amount of narcotics you were likely to get fired. In the Robert Stigwood Organisation of the 1960s, we artists would phone in our drug requirements each Wednesday to the accounts department in the Stigwood office on Upper Brook Street, in London's Mayfair. By Friday lunchtime, little brown envelopes with each artist's name on them were awaiting us in the office. The envelopes contained the drugs, which Stigwood's people organised. They did this so that artists minimised the risk of arrest by cutting out the need to buy the illegal substances ourselves. Stigwood did not involve himself in the supplying of the drugs to artists, indeed he probably didn't know what was taking place in his HQ. At that time, Stigwood had not been seen in the office for some months following a strange incident involving the disappearance of a large amount of cash and the instant dismissal of a number of employees.

Stigwood became the manager of numerous artists – Eric Clapton among them – after he teamed up with the Gunnell brothers, Rick and John, who emerged from London's underworld to occupy a place at the top of the new music movement being created in the 1960s. They ran a booking agency and brought to Robert Stigwood (whose main stars at the time were the Bee Gees) muscle, expertise and quite a number of artists.

The Gunnell brothers also ran late-night clubs which were all the rage in 'Swinging London', and featured live bands as well as loud recorded music. The most famous was the Bag O Nails, situated on Kingly Street in London's fashionable Soho district (later renamed the Val Bonne). In those days, Kingly Street was a seedy back street but it was just around the corner from Carnaby Street, which at the time was the centre of the world. The Gunnells in no small measure helped shape the modern music industry. The business was not the squeaky-clean, well-ordered operation it is today. It was anarchic and anti-establishment and anything seemed possible. It was the Gunnell brothers who, through their underlings in the Stigwood organisation, looked after our narco-needs. And believe me, we appreciated it.

Walter Yetnikoff embraced the spirit of the times. Moreover, he took that spirit to unprecedented levels. While he was doing this both he and his artists prospered. But when he got religion he put himself beyond the pale. His colleagues found it difficult to deal with the totality of the change Yetnikoff underwent. In addition, perhaps Yetnikoff himself failed to understand the impact his sudden conversion would have on those around him. And he was just as extreme in his new mindset as he was in his old one.

Eventually, Norio Ohga summoned Yetnikoff to his office on the top floor of Sony's New York headquarters. The large, rectangular room incorporated a beautiful vista of Manhattan. At the far end of the office, beyond two of the plushest sofas imaginable, was Ohga's desk, which itself was about the size of a football pitch. There were two pictures on Ohga's walls. They were not Picasso's or anything like that, which is surprising given Ohga's cultured personality. One was a nondescript depiction of the building in which they were sitting, while the other was a similar drab sketch of Sony's headquarters in Japan. As Yetnikoff entered, Ohga stood up and the man who had been responsible for some of the world's greatest musical recordings of the twentieth century was summarily fired. 'This hurts me more than it hurts you,' Ohga lied, 'The board has decided you need a sabbatical.' Yetnikoff tells what happened next. After Ohga left the room, a security guard asked Yetnikoff to leave the building by a side exit. 'Later I learned it (the order to leave by the side exit) was because in the adjoining room Ohga was meeting with Mottola and already planning the new regime.' There was to be no sabbatical, Yetnikoff was out.

After Yetnikoff was fired, he went to lunch with an old CBS executive he had known for years. The following day, Yetnikoff received a call from Mickey Schulhof, for a long time Sony's main US lawyer and the first non-Japanese appointed to Sony's board of directors. 'Your severance agreement,' he told the bemused Yetnikoff, 'forbids you from discussing the music business with former employees.' Yetnikoff was dismissive of Schulhof's threats and carried on regardless. This event would be mirrored fifteen years later when Paul Russell gave the *Mail on Sunday* the story of Michael Jackson's finances and received a warning letter from Sony's lawyers telling him to keep his mouth shut. So when Norio Ohga and Akio Morita began their determined and patient campaign against Michael Jackson some five years after the Yetnikoff episode, it was not behaviour against type. On the contrary, it was merely a continuation of the same pattern, only the target was different.

Another example of Sony's sharp practices can be seen in the case of Steve Popovich, who brought Meat Loaf to CBS and was instrumental in securing the signature of Michael Jackson. Popovich claimed that CBS had not paid him full royalties on the Meat Loaf deal and so wanted an audit. Unfortunately for Popovich, the relevant clause in the contract meant he was out of time. Walter Yetnikoff, who believed Popovich had a good case, gave him a waiver so he could carry out the audit. In the meantime, Sony bought CBS and in due course, Yetnikoff was fired. When Popovich introduced his waiver, Sony refused to recognise it. Popovich sued. Yetnikoff states that Sony's approach was to declare full-scale war on Popovich 'Giant Sony attempts to crush little Stevie Popovich,' is how Yetnikoff tells it. Eventually, as the company has often done, Sony settled the case on the courthouse steps.

There is a coda to the Yetnikoff story. The former executive was so annoyed by Schulhof's attempts to shut him up that he told Sony to sue him. 'Of course they never did,' Yetnikoff said. 'And I suspect, given their fear of what I know, they never will.' Yetnikoff has never answered the question this statement begs. What, exactly, is it that he knows? Whatever it is, it must be of such a magnitude as to make his former employers fearful. Yetnikoff knows how Sony operates. For instance, he introduces the subject of what he knows in the context of litigation, when he told

Schulhof to sue him. This is code. Sony never backed out of legal disputes. The company might settle a case on the steps of the court but those in charge were never afraid of getting stuck-in to a lawsuit. The entertainment division of the Sony Corporation is packed with lawyers. Yetnikoff is telling us that Sony altered its ethos and *modus operandi* rather than face the consequences if the record executive went public.

Norio Ohga became the undisputed head of the Sony Corporation in 1989 following the acquisitions of CBS and Columbia Pictures. His elevation came as Morita gradually withdrew and Kazuo Iwama started the long descent into corporate oblivion. Ohga now possessed the supreme title: President and Chief Executive Officer. Morita was given the kiss-of-death job, revered Chairman of the Board. Ohga knew his sacred duty was to carry the company born out of the ashes of 1945 into the 21st century, intact and prospering. At first it seemed like a stick-on. Then came the Chandler affair. Music, the art form closest to his heart and the driving force of his vision for Sony's future, had turned into Ohga's tainted love.

Michael Jackson was one of the main reasons Sony bought CBS in the first place. Sony's motivation in acquiring the giant US record label lay in the debacle the company experienced in the video wars of the 1970s and 80s. There was no question that Sony had produced the best system; its Betamax product. However, the company lost out to the rival VHS system because more software – that is, films and other pre-recorded tapes – was available in the VHS format. Sony, which thought that the main usage of video tape recorders would be for recording television programmes, was severely caught out and Betamax proved a very expensive failure. This taught those at Sony, who were essentially engineers, the true value of copyright ownership and the software that can flow from such ownership. Software, as they now saw, equalled profits.

So the purchases of CBS records and Columbia Pictures were designed to ensure that whatever new formats might be introduced in the future (and the commercial DVD was not far away), Sony would not be found wanting again. But this objective depended on retaining ownership rights for a long period of time, preferably in perpetuity. That was because everything could always be repackaged and sold in whatever formats might be invented in the future, but only if you retained ownership of the rights. In the record business, the ownership of a sound recording is essential and is known as the mechanical copyright.

Sometimes, being in the right place at the right time is everything. This is especially true in show business where there are many talented artists and producers, most of whom never attain the recognition they deserve. I have known a prolific writer, producer and manager for almost forty years called Philip Bailey, who uses the name PHAB in the music business. Bailey had been trying for many years to realise a decent amount of money from his activities. He wrote and recorded a number of what I believed were great songs, some of which were produced by Jimmy Edwards and myself.

By the 1980s, Bailey had achieved some reasonable successes but was always chasing what he termed 'The big one'. Bailey prided himself (and still does) on never getting out of bed before midday. He would often then while away the afternoon driving from his home in Surrey to record company offices in central London, where he would shoot the breeze and look for new deals. One day, he was in the office of a record company called Telstar, which specialised in tele-marketing. Telstar had been working for some months on a project with the cigarette manufacturer, Benson and Hedges. With the government beginning to pass legislation banning cigarette advertising, the tobacco companies were looking at other ways to promote their products. Benson and Hedges decided to place vouchers in cigarette packets which could be redeemed at record shops for a special album of classic soul music tracks, one that could not be purchased without the vouchers. Telstar had approached Warner Brothers, which owned the mechanical copyright to a number of old soul hits. Warners agreed to supply the music and Telstar thought they had a deal.

On the afternoon PHAB entered Telstar's office, all hell had broken loose. A couple of hours earlier, Warners had announced that they were pulling out of the deal, as they didn't want to be associated with cigarettes or alcohol. The Telstar executives were dumbfounded at the turn of events and they saw their lucrative B&H contract disappearing before their eyes. Bailey told me what happened next.

'I had licenced some copyrights some time previously which included some soul tracks by the Chi-Lites, Jackie Wilson, Curtis Mayfield and Sam and Dave,' he said. 'So I said to Telstar that I could supply them with an album. They looked at me like I was their saviour. They asked me to go straight home, put together the best of what I had and they would present it to Benson's the next day.' Telstar were as good as their word and Benson and Hedges agreed the content of the new compilation. A production run of 100,000 CDs was agreed. So pleased were Telstar with their saviour that they paid Bailey $150,000 up front. It was the 'big one' and from there, Bailey never looked back. Indeed he went out the next day and splashed out on a new, fully loaded BMW eight series, which he owns to this day. I have to say that it couldn't have happened to a nicer guy and everyone who knew PHAB was extremely pleased for him. Apart from an object lesson in the importance of being in the right place at the right time, this story reveals how ownership of or licence rights to mechanical copyright can provide success on a scale most can only dream about.

Mechanical copyright ownership has been a thorny issue in the record industry for many years. Generally, record companies do everything they can to own the copyright, while artists, who have often borne the cost of recordings from advances handed out by the record company and recouped before royalties are paid, believe they should, at some point, own their own recordings. In the 1960s, virtually all artist deals gave the record company the mechanical copyright forever. By the 1970s, with the advent of super-groups and sharp music business lawyers and managers, some companies recognised the need for change.

It was in this spirit that Paul Russell and some other enlightened music business executives decided they must negotiate more equitable contracts with their artists. At CBS a formula was developed called a 'Dunkirk Clause', which enabled artists, at the end of the contractual period, to gain ownership of the mechanical copyright of their recordings. Michael Jackson's contract with CBS contained such a Dunkirk Clause and it remained intact when the contract was renegotiated with Sony in 1991.

'Thriller' was, of course, CBS's biggest seller ever and other Jackson albums such as 'Bad' were not far behind. If Sony tried to get rid of Jackson, the terms of the contract between the parties meant that a messy legal case which would cost Sony dear would ensue. Worse than that from Sony's point of view was the possibility of Jackson removing the mechanical copyright of his recordings from Sony's control if they made any mistakes. At a stroke, a guaranteed revenue stream stretching way into the future would be under threat. So those at Sony had to find a way to rid the company of Jackson but keep hold of the rights to his record-ings. There was also the matter of Sony ATV, in which the Japanese were determined to acquire a controlling interest. Even Norio Ohga could not have envisaged it would take ten years, a high-profile criminal trial and the personal destruction of one of music's greatest ever talents before the objective was finally realised.

6

HISTORY AND BLOOD

Tommy Mottola was between a rock and a hard place. Michael Jackson had emerged from the Jordan Chandler affair as damaged goods and Mottola had to brief Norio Ohga about the extent to which Jackson was tarnishing the Sony name in the USA. Ohga, for his part, made clear to Mottola his displeasure that Jackson was associated with Sony at all. Mottola, however, also had to sell records and keep artists, including Michael Jackson, happy. The result was 'HIStory', a strange double CD hybrid comprising some greatest hits along with fifteen new songs (one of them being 'D.S.', the song about Tom Sneddon). It was a format that was always going to be difficult to market effectively. Perhaps that was the aim.

Against all odds, 'HIStory' provided Jackson and Sony with one of their fastest-selling singles ever. 'You Are Not Alone', went to number one on the US Billboard chart in its first week of release. 'HIStory' sold over fifteen million copies world-wide, an amazing amount for any performer – except Michael Jackson. For him, it was the worst sales performance since 'Off The Wall' first announced him as a major solo artist. 'Off The Wall' also sold fifteen million but in contrast to 'HIStory' it was seen at the time as a rip-roaring success. 'Thriller', of course, hit the fifty million plus mark, 'Bad' managed twenty-five million, as did 'Dangerous'. To provide some perspective I looked at the sales figures of a CD by a different artist during the same period. I wanted something which was widely regarded as a great success. At random I chose the debut album by Men At Work, the Australian band whose most well-known song was the blockbuster hit 'Down Under'. The album shifted eighteen million copies. Thus Jackson's sales of 'HIStory' were well within the boundaries of what was deemed successful, yet by his own standards it could be perceived, not least by himself, as a dismal failure.

This outcome was a double-edged sword for Tommy Mottola. On the one hand, having helped oust the iconic Walter Yetnikoff from Sony, he had to prove himself within the record industry as someone who could match Yetnikoff's ratio of hits. On the other, he was in thrall to the man who promoted and protected him, Norio Ohga. And Ohga, along with Akio Morita, required Mottola's contribution to the bigger picture

Mottola was known in the music busness primarily as a manager of artists. He had a short-lived career as a singer called J.D. Valentine and while at the microphone did well enough to get a record contract with, ironically, CBS's Epic label. He was born in the Bronx and always retained the image of a typical New York Italian-American. He even went to the extent of creating an aura around himself which said he just might have underworld connections. The truth is his father was a customs broker who did well enough to move the family to the more affluent suburb of New Rochelle, where the young Tommy Mottola learned to play the trumpet and the guitar. In 1971, he married Lisa Clark, whose father, Sam, founded ABC Records and was a big mover in the US music industry. During his courtship of Lisa, Mottola gave up Catholicism and converted to Judaism, his new wife's religion.

As a manager, Mottola made his name with the duo Hall & Oates, who had a string of hits from the early 1970s to the millennium and whose album, 'Abandoned Luncheonette' remains a classic to this day. In an extraordinary deal, Mottola owned the name, had all his expenses paid and took 25% of all profits. Daryl Hall and John Oates' share was $500,000 of debts, to RCA Records and the US Internal Revenue Service.

Mottola's company at the time was called Don Tommy Enterprises (note the use of the cosa nostra inspired word, 'Don') but he soon changed that to Champion, where he numbered Carly Simon and John Mellenkamp among his managerial clients. Not long after Walter Yetnikoff appointed him head of the US record labels, Mottola met then wooed a girl singer he had encountered at a party. Her name was Mariah Carey and soon she and Mottola embarked on an affair which culminated, first in Mottola's divorce from Lisa (he cited 'cultural differences' in the papers), then in a star-studded wedding to Mariah Carey, attended by the likes of Bruce Springsteen, Barbara Steisand, Robert De Niro and Ozzy Osbourne. Meanwhile, Mottola gave Carey a huge recording contract with Sony. Her debut album, released in 1990, sold some eight million copies.

Mottola and Carey separated in 1997 and divorced in 1998. Mariah Carey left Sony in 2001 complaining of similar promotional problems to those which so irritated George Michael and Michael Jackson. By then, Mottola was Chairman and CEO of Sony Music Entertainment USA. In the video for 'Honey', a track on Mariah Carey's comeback album, 'Butterfly', the singer is seen escaping from imprisonment by a gangster-like character, finally achieving freedom, despite suffering close calls in her persecutor's attempts to thwart her ambition.

During his time at Sony, Mottola seems to have specialized in young women singers and songwriters. Celine Dion, Jennifer Lopez and Béyonce Knowles (along with her original group, Destiny's Child); all were signed to Sony on Mottola's watch. He also had an affair with a Japanese singer who was Akio Morita's god-daughter.

Running a record label is entirely different to management, however. There is a constant pressure to find the next genius and improve the bottom line. There is also the politics of a multi-national, from which Mottola benefited when he helped in the regicide of Walter Yetnikoff. Now, Norio Ohga let Mottola know exactly what he thought about Michael Jackson. In addition to all of this, Mottola was supposed to find new artists for the record label and that particular part of his job was not going to plan. Sony Records was simply not performing as well as it had under the mercurial Yetnikoff, not least because it was impossible to reproduce the profits of 'Thriller'. Many years later, Mottola had this to say about his personality during those years. 'I was a hustler, a guy who thought he knew it all. I was hungry, I was ambitious, I was anxious, I was raging. Budda-bump, budda-bump, budda-bump.'

Michael Jackson's contract with Sony contained obligations on the singer's part to deliver finished CD's. There was also a requirement that over the period of the contract – which ended up being fifteen years – the sum of all the songs on all the CD's reached a minimum number. This clause was included to avoid the possibility of the artist recording one long song and calling it a CD. It was, if you will, a sort of insurance policy. Sony also had certain rights to repackage Jackson's back catalogue. Their rights were strong but not absolute, so any greatest hits compilation had in practice to be agreed between Sony and Jackson. Half of 'HIStory' was old songs. My information has it that Sony, after the Chandler affair, wanted to release a single CD of Jackson's greatest hits, while Jackson insisted on a batch of new songs. The double CD was the messy result. It did, however, alert the powers that be at Sony Records, led by Tommy Mottola, to the fact that they could use contractual requirements in their agreement with Jackson for their own purposes, in the process making some decisions which on the face of it appear totally bizarre.

In 1997, only two years after 'HIStory', Sony released an even stranger hybrid CD, 'Blood on the Dance Floor – HIStory in the mix'. Before recording started on the album, Sony had invoked its right to ten new songs. Jackson, though, did not agree with Sony's interpretation of their contract. After intense negotiations with Jackson's advisors, a compromise was reached which resulted in the CD containing five new songs plus eight remixes of tracks from 'HIStory'. However, what seems to be a normal negotiating process was actually part of the campaign to manipulate Jackson in the interests of Sony, not the singer's own career. Usually, the interests of the artist and the record label coincide, or if they don't, they should. In the case of Jackson and Sony, they were now massively divergent.

Tommy Mottola made it clear to Jackson that Sony were demanding ten new songs, knowing that Jackson, who was already experiencing a different attitude from his record company than he had enjoyed in the past, would resist. It was always a ploy of Jackson's to make statements of his power by refusing to do things other artists would routinely perform, mainly on a whim or when he believed matters were not going his way. His request for Walter Yetnikoff over the 'Days of Thunder' song was a case in point. Another example of this behaviour occurred when Jackson starred in a short movie, produced by George Lucas and funded by the Disney Corporation to the tune of $21 million for twenty minutes of screen time. Authorised personally by Disney's boss, Michael Eisner, it was a space epic called *Captain Eo*, made in 3D and shown exclusively in specially constructed theatres in Disney theme parks in California, Florida and France. It featured much singing, dancing and special effects with a sort-of plot which saw a spaceship commander, Captain Eo (Jackson), saving the world from the forces of evil. I saw it in Paris and it was an impressive spectacle. The 3D effects were sensational and Jackson's singing and dancing, in my opinion, reached new heights. To my mind, the movie has never received the acclaim I believe it deserves.

Furthermore, *Captain Eo* pioneered a completely new way of producing and marketing a movie by creating a symbiosis between three discrete entertainment forms. There has long been a fusion between two of them, music and film, but *Captain Eo*, a musical and visual extravaganza, was placed in, indeed specifically created for a third element, the fastest-growing experiential entertainment medium of the era – the theme park.

The movie's very innovation meant it represented something of a gamble on the part of Disney. Not unnaturally, Disney's marketing people thought Jackson would make personal appearances at the American parks to help promote the new attraction. After all, one of them, Disneyland, was just down the road in California. However, Jackson, the self-styled children's advocate, refused, on the basis that if he were to be seen alongside Mickey Mouse *et al.*, he would be mistaken for a children's entertainer. This is so obviously ridiculous as to be beyond rational comment. Eventually, Walter Yetnikoff brokered a half-baked solution of partial promotion that satisfied nobody.

So Sony understood perfectly well that Jackson would at first refuse to do something by denying any contractual obligation but would then reach a compromise. Jackson would see this as a victory, since what had been originally demanded was modified after the singer made his opposition known. It's a device many stars employ to feed their egos but Jackson took it to new heights. Now it was being used against him. So when five new songs and eight remixes were agreed for 'Blood on the Dance Floor', Jackson thought he had outsmarted the suits. It was a huge mistake. In his professional career it would prove the turning point towards complete disaster. To release a CD with only five new songs coupled with remixes from a batch of recordings released only two years previously confused the record-buying public, particularly in America. Jackson would have been better served remixing 'Thriller' and waiting to release a CD full of new songs. It was half-assed Michael Jackson, almost as if he couldn't be bothered to produce a whole new CD. Jackson CDs before 'Blood on the Dance Floor' were eagerly awaited, in part because music fans knew that there would be at least six or seven new songs which would become classics. Moreover, Jackson was no longer the young kid on the block. Pop music always changes and a new generation was reinventing American music through hip-hop and rap. Jackson was ideally placed to go with this flow because of his pioneering approach in the 1980s. But he had to be on top of his game and committed, otherwise he would get left behind. At this stage, Jackson also began to take full credit for his previous successes.

He would often, say, for instance, that the producer of 'Thriller', the great Quincy Jones, had not, in fact, contributed much to his music. This flew in the face of the facts. Jones, one of the great musical talents of all time, was as responsible for Jackson's unique sound as the singer himself.

'Blood on the Dance Floor', while providing some brilliant moments, simply did not contain enough new material to excite people. No one was interested in remixes of tracks which were only two years old anyway. The remixes themselves in the main sounded tired and complacent. It was a record which a source within Sony told me 'No record company could market properly'. Those at Sony, especially Tommy Mottola, must have known this, even more so after his experience with 'HIStory', which at least had a reasonable complement of new songs.

None of this, of course, could be made public. Sony had to be seen to be supporting Jackson with marketing dollars. Record labels owe a duty of care to artists and they should conduct their business properly, otherwise they could be in breach of contract. They should certainly not attempt to sabotage the career of one of their artists. The truth was that anyone with a passing knowledge of the recent history of popular music, let alone executives in a multi-national corporation, would know that the only way to get Michael Jackson's career back up to its previous position post-Chandler was to concentrate on Jackson's strengths, which were considerable. As Paul Russell said much later, 'A completely new album of great songs, not overproduced but showcasing Michael's voice, allied to a world tour, would have done the trick and the same is true now (2005).' Jackson was never encouraged to do this by his management or record company. I believe that by then, the King of Pop was too far gone to remember what made him great in the first place.

In some territories, 'Blood on the Dance Floor' was reasonably successful, most notably in Britain, where the CD's title song was an instant hit. However, the British market, while important, particularly in terms of prestige and world-wide influence, is not big enough by itself to sustain a career on the level of Jackson's. Consequently, world sales of the CD were a pathetic four million, a real disaster for Michael Jackson, as opposed to the self-perceived disasters of his previous three recordings. Its failure also boosted Sony's opinion about the chances of the ultimate success of their strategy and convinced them they were on the right track. And although Jackson moaned incessantly to Tommy Mottola and

Michael Jackson performs on stage with the Jackson Five during the Jackson 5 Victory Tour at Arrowhead Stadium, Kansas City on 6th July 1984. (Photo by Dave Hogan/Getty Images)

Sony ATV was originally formed under the name Associated Television (ATV) in the UK during the 1950s. It was founded by one of Britain's greatest impresarios, Lew Grade.
(Photo by Peter Cade/Central Press/Getty Images)

This picture dated 20th October 1992, shows Akio Morita (Left), the business tycoon who co-founded the electronics giant Sony Corporation, and his partner Masaru Ibuka. Ibuka and Morita came up with a corporate philosophy which transferred the allegiance of the Japanese worker from old and discredited institutions to the new corporations. These companies would be the saviours of Japan and the redeemers of its national pride. Every area of a worker's life was to be designed around the notion that employees should subsume individuality for the corporate good. Morita and Ibuka created the Japanese model, copied not only in Japan itself but eventually all around the globe. By that time, however, the Japanese had already changed the world. (Photo: AFP/Getty Images)

The catalyst for Michael Jackson's 2005 trial was the television programme, 'Living with Michael Jackson', made by the British journalist, Martin Bashir, and which was broadcast in February 2003. When the programme was aired in the USA, 27 million people tuned in, while an astonishing 14 million watched the British screening. These numbers were replicated all over the world. (Photo by Win McNamee/Getty Images)

On 27th March, Michael Jackson gave an extensive interview to Revd Jesse Jackson for the reverend's internet radio show, where the two Jacksons discussed Michael's financial situation. Michael Jackson did not deny the story. Instead he said: 'This is tabloid sensationalism kind of gossip'. To that Jesse Jackson replied: 'Some people called and they thought it was about the Sony catalogue'. Jesse Jackson pressed the issue: 'It was suggested by a number of your friends this fight was really about this catalogue issue'. It was the first time anyone had come so close to the truth. (Photo by Bob Falcetti/Getty Images)

OJ Simpson, the star running back of the Buffalo Bills, was found not guilty of murdering his wife and her friend. What was surprising was the reaction, especially in the USA, from the public and the media. It appeared that white Americans were convinced Simpson was guilty, whereas African-Americans believed in his innocence. The media were as one: Simpson did it and had gotten away with murder. It was not long before Simpson found himself persona non grata in the USA. Similar to OJ Simpson, Michael Jackson found out that a not guilty verdict does not an innocent man make in the eyes of commentators and consequently, the public. (Photo by Wilfredo Lee/Getty Images)

Tom Sneddon's final witness was someone he believed would end his case with a bang. It was Debbie Rowe, the mother of Jackson's two children and the singer's ex-wife. Sneddon, knowing that Rowe and Jackson had not always been the happy couple, believed Rowe would attack Jackson on the stand. However, Rowe was a disaster for Sneddon and as she was his last witness, it was difficult for him to recover his position. 'We've been friends and we were married,' Rowe told the court. She went on to say that the pair had known each other for over twenty years before they were married. Then she dropped her bombshell. She praised Jackson as a parent and said any problems in his life were caused by the hangers-on surrounding the singer. 'Vultures' she called them.
(Photo by Aaron Lambert/AFP/Getty Images)Getty Images)

'Tommy Mottola,' Jackson said, 'is mean, racist and very, very devilish'.
These words travelled around the world in double-quick time.
Tommy mottola was head of Sony's US record division. While Mottola was not the most popular record company executive in the world, those working inside the building simply couldn't comprehend what was going on. One of them said that they 'dismissed it as a joke. It just showed that Michael (Jackson) had finally "lost it" '. (Photo by Evan Agostini/Getty Images)

Michael Jackson waves to fans as he arrives for court on 17th September 2004 in Santa Maria, California.
The area where Michael Jackson did take Sneddon on was in the realm of public relations. This is Jackson's natural territory and he wiped the floor with the DA, who couldn't help but come across as sanctimonious, smug and ever-so-slightly unstable. Even when Jackson did something outrageous, like standing on the roof of his car to entertain the crowd after one of the preliminary hearings, it worked in his favour, invoking first incredulity, then confirmation of our belief that Michael Jackson – aka Jacko – is, well, weird. And who can forget the time he arrived in court in his pyjamas after the drama of the bad back and the visit to the emergency room? Tom Sneddon stood no chance. (Photo by Doug Benc/Getty Images)

*Jackson's defence attorney, the silvery-maned Tom Mesereau claimed all along that the whole case was a scam
to obtain a large sum of money from Michael Jackson. The architect of the scam, according to Mesereau,
was Janet Arvizo, who coached her children to lie as part of her plan. (Photo by Mark Mainz/Getty Images)*

Tom 'Mad Dog' Sneddon (centre), and his assistants, Ron Zonen (left), and Gordon Auchincloss (right), who were in charge of the prosecution case, seemed addicted to overkill. Thwarted ten years earlier in his attempt to convict Michael Jackson of child sexual abuse, after 'Living with Michael Jackson' hit the world's television screens, Thomas W. Sneddon Jr believed his chance for payback had finally arrived. (Photo Mario Anzuoni/AFP/Getty Images)

Norio Ohga became President and Chief Executive Officer of Sony in 1989.
Ohga was one of the main players in Sony Corporation's quest for the ultimate acquisition: What Sony wanted at the end of it all was ownership of Jackson's back catalogue, including 'Thriller'. To achieve this it would be necessary eventually, to destroy Jackson's career.
(Photo: Toshifumi Kitamura /AFP/ Getty Images)

Just as 'Living with Michael Jackson' was broadcast Ohga retired as Chairman of the Board and apart from overseeing the Jackson business his role became ceremonial. In the latter days of Ohga's rule and later, under the auspices of Idei, Sony was no longer the force it had once been and was in no position to turn itself around. In response, the board took the momentous decision to give the top job to a non-Japanese for the first time. Sir Howard Stringer, a Welsh-American who had run the US Entertainment division, assumed the mantle of leader. (Photo Yoshikazu Tsuno/AFP/Getty Images)

Tom Sneddon, the lawyer for the prosecution is widely believed to be the inspiration for the Michael Jackson song, 'D.S.', which appeared on the 'HIStory' album of 1996. The song rubbed salt into the wounds Sneddon sustained when he failed to force Jackson into court in 1994. Above, Michael Jackson performs on stage during his "HiStory" concert tour held in New York in 1997 (Photo by Dave Hogan/Getty Images)

'HIStory' provided Jackson and Sony with one of their fastest-selling singles ever. 'You Are Not Alone', went to number one on the US Billboard chart in its first week of release. 'HIStory' sold over fifteen million copies world-wide. NEW YORK. 1997 : Michael Jackson performing on stage during his "HIStory" concert tour held in New York in 1997.(Photo by Dave Hogan/Getty Images)

'Not Guilty.' Again and again these two little words from the voice of the jury foreman, Paul Rodriguez, reverberated around the courtroom. There was one count of conspiracy to kidnap and falsely imprison an entire family, four counts of committing lewd acts, one count of attempting to commit a lewd act, four counts of supplying alcohol to minors and a number of counts on lesser charges arising from the same crimes, allegedly committed against an underage boy, Gavin Arvizo. These last counts were offered to the jury as alternatives should they find the accused innocent of the main indictments. Instead, they found the defendant not guilty on all charges.
(Photo by Carlo Allegri/Getty Images)

anyone else that would listen about Sony's performance, his complaints were seen as sour grapes. All the blame for the fiasco was poured onto Jackson's head. The CD was a major failure in the USA, where the media had been waiting for a substandard Jackson CD in order to be able to divine some moral equivalence between Jackson's alleged behaviour and his creative output. They thought they could do it with 'HIStory' but 'Blood on the Dance Floor' gave them the perfect opportunity. Just desserts and all that.

In J. Randy Taraborrelli's biography, *The Magic and the Madness* the author claims that the relative failure of 'Blood on the Dance Floor' changed Sony's view of Michael Jackson. 'It should … be noted that it was because of its weak showing Sony executives no longer viewed Michael as being "invincible"', Taraborrelli writes. 'Heads would not roll, it was learned, if he had a flop record, or if he was unhappy with the company. After 'Blood on the Dance Floor' disappointed in the USA, he (Jackson) was never a company priority again.'

Despite the excellence of most of Taraborrelli's analysis elsewhere in his book, he cannot be expected to understand the machinations, especially those ostensibly based around technical issues, which go on inside record companies. My point is that far from being surprised by the sales of 'Blood on the Dance Floor' and reacting to them, Sony engineered the outcome from the outset. Not only that, Taraborrelli might be right in the conventional sense when he states that Michael Jackson was 'never a priority again,' but in fact Jackson remained an extremely high priority for Sony. Not, as was customary, to help sell records, but to get rid of the singer while gaining control of his back catalogue and, most importantly, acquiring a controlling interest in Sony ATV. To achieve that objective Jackson had to fail in a way that enabled Sony to appear blameless. Once 'Blood on the Dance Floor' bombed, the company could justify any spending decisions as simply a reaction to Jackson's new market position.

The sales performance of 'Blood on the Dance Floor' opened the door to a further opportunity to allow certain of Michael Jackson's character traits to hasten his downfall. Another front in the battle was about to be opened up.

It is well known that Jackson is a spender on a legendary scale. The shopping, Neverland, the zoo, the fun-fair in his grounds, various up-market properties, all and more do not have to be documented to any great extent here. However, for big-time celebrities, shopping often fulfils some deeper need than appears to be the case at first sight. In the late 1960s, I became friends with one of the Bee Gees, the late, lamented Maurice Gibb. Maurice was the most underrated of the Gibb brothers but he provided the glue which kept them together. The twins, Barry and Robin, were often at loggerheads with each other and always seemed to be competing for the accolades that came the Bee Gees' way. Maurice would, on those occasions, find himself in the middle and was forced to play the role of peacemaker. Towards the end of the 1960s even Maurice couldn't keep his fractious brothers together. Matters came to a head when Robert Stigwood chose one of Barry's songs, 'First of May' to be the A-side of a single, in preference to one of Robin's. As a consequence, the Bee Gees actually split up for a short time.

Maurice thought he had found his own niche in life when he married the singer Lulu, who had an international hit singing the title song to the movie, 'To Sir With Love'. Unfortunately, like many showbiz marriages, the union was ill-starred. As their relationship began to fall apart, Maurice sought solace in shopping. Whenever he returned to the UK from a tour he would be laden with the latest consumer goods which he would bring to show me. He did not do this to flaunt his wealth, he was a friendly, lovely man who managed to retain a degree of modesty almost unknown in the mad world of 1960s pop music.

One day, Jimmy Edwards and I were in the Phonogram (a subsidiary of Philips) recording studio in London, cutting some tracks with the producer, Mike Hurst. Hurst had discovered and produced Cat Stevens, having started his professional career as one of the Springfields, a vocal group of the early sixties which first showcased the singing talent of perhaps the greatest female vocalist ever to come out of these islands, Dusty Springfield. The Springfields were responsible for one of my all-time favourite songs, 'Island of Dreams'. As the recording session was reaching its critical point, we were interrupted by a beaming Maurice Gibb, who bounded into the studio with the enthusiasm of a small boy. 'Lynton, come with me,' he said. 'Just a minute', I replied, rather brusquely, as my attention was focused on the job in hand. 'No, you don't understand', Maurice went on, 'come here, follow me'. Something in Maurice's voice told me it was important, so Jimmy and I dropped what we were doing and followed Maurice, who conspiratorially tip-toed out of the studio.

When we reached the street, Maurice stood there with his arms outstretched towards the road and said: 'What do you think of that?' He directed our gaze to the kerb. Our eyes widened. There, in all its glory, stood a beautiful, immaculate Bentley Continental convertible automobile, cherry red, with its top down. It must have cost a king's ransom. 'Fancy a spin?' Maurice said. He didn't have to ask twice. His question needed no answer. With all thoughts of the recording session forgotten, we piled into the Bentley. Maurice got behind the wheel and off we went, to Kings Road in Chelsea, where we spent the afternoon posing.

Really, Maurice had bought the car to somehow assuage the pain of his failing marital relationship. Don't get me wrong, Maurice was as excited as we were, maybe more so. But shopping on a mammoth scale was his way – along with the consumption of copious amounts of alcohol – of calming his mind amid the turmoil in his life which stemmed from the situation with Lulu and his relationship with his brothers.

I do not know what pain Michael Jackson needed to dull. There have obviously been episodes in his life which he prefers to submerge. Like Maurice Gibb, though, he saw spending as his way out of some sort of depressive tendency. But also like Maurice Gibb, it didn't work. Someone who observed Jackson close up over a number of years told me that by far the greatest drain on the singer's resources was the business organisation, with its massive and expensive workforce, that Jackson draped around himself after 'Thriller'. The problem was that to sustain the operation over time a Thriller-type level of ongoing income was constantly required.

There is no question that the success of 'Thriller' went to Jackson's head. He was totally convinced his future records would sell even more than his masterpiece. Although the professional record people around Jackson knew perfectly well that the success of 'Thriller' could never be repeated, no one saw fit to explain this to Jackson. Instead, his illusions were indulged. Neither did Jackson want to hear any contradictions to his opinion that the follow-up to 'Thriller' would sell 100 million. Walter Yetnikoff found ever more inventive ways to avoid telling Jackson the bald truth. 'You keep touring, 'Bad' will keep selling,' was Yetnikoff's last, feeble attempt. For Michael Jackson to have cut down on his entourage was unthinkable. It would be an admission of defeat. For Jackson, maintaining the unreal at any cost was far more important than acknowledging anything even remotely approaching actuality. It was his very identity that was at stake.

In fact, with proper management and support from his record label, Jackson could have kept his lifestyle, and thus his illusions, intact. When appearing live, for instance, despite the staggering overheads, Jackson could clear $1 million profit per concert, even after the Chandler settlement, which, let's not forget, cost Jackson many millions of dollars, both in payments to Jordan Chandler and associated legal, PR and other expenses.

A friend of mine, Barrie Barlow, who was the drummer with Jethro Tull in their heyday, received hardly any income from the band's record sales. He nevertheless managed to buy a beautiful house on the River Thames at Lower Shiplake, near Henley in Oxfordshire, from his share of the proceeds of Tull gigs played mainly in US stadia. He later converted the outhouses into a superb recording studio called The Doghouse, which still produces great sounds to the present day. Live performances can be extremely lucrative for the right artist. Jackson ticked all the boxes.

What Jackson needed was a professional strategy to rehabilitate himself in the eyes of the public, especially in his homeland. Instead, he received the opposite. The star did little to help himself during this period and was in no mood to accept any advice that differed from his own views. So far removed was he from his own personality, Jackson began to fire anyone who contradicted him, no matter how long they had been at his side, nor how important their role might be. Meanwhile, outgoings were rising as income was falling. Sony did nothing, which had the effect of stoking the fires.

As the millennium approached, Jackson's royalties, although still considerable, were hit by the poor performance of 'Blood on the Dance Floor'. There was income from the old material but lucrative sponsorship contracts and profitable tours were a thing of the past. Jackson saw no need to reduce staff numbers so salary costs spiralled upwards. And the fantasy world that was Neverland continued to require large amounts of funding. But that was only the beginning: there was also a travelling circus led by Jackson and Lisa-Marie Presley and the star was bankrolling his extended family. Soon there would be a new partner, Debbie Rowe, and two children of their own. He was forced to start eating into his capital.

Before long, a huge hole began to appear in Michael Jackson's finances. Once created, the deficit grew exponentially. While this was going on, Jackson was arguing with just about everybody, including Sony. According to *The Magic and the Madness*, Jackson and his advisors misunderstood the terms of the singer's contract with Sony. I do not know whether J. Randy Taraborrelli read the contract himself to verify the claims he makes in his book. If he did it must be a different contract from the one to which I had access. From the nature of the assertions in the book, which, quite frankly, are so ludicrous as to be impossible to believe, it is highly unlikely that Taraborrelli ever set eyes on the clauses in the contract which were relevant to the points he raises.

In 1998 Michael Jackson began working on a completely new set of songs, eventually released under the title 'Invincible' in 2001. The first thing Taraborrelli says about this is that Sony paid Jackson some $40 million to cover recording costs, which would be recouped by the record label from Jackson's royalties. Taraborrelli goes on: 'They (Sony) then spent another twenty-five million (dollars) to promote it (though, it's difficult to specify how these funds were allocated because the promotion was so weak)'. Exactly how much the recordings cost is lost in the mists of time. The figure of $40 million for recording 'Invincible' was a figure given to the press to be spun as the costliest album in the history of the universe.

It is doubtful whether the bills for recording the new CD were anything like the reported numbers. Since all we have to go on is the hype, it is impossible to know what the actual cost was. My best guess is that it came to half the reported figure. Perhaps more important is the statement that Sony handed over $40 million to Jackson as an advance to pay for the recording. This sounds completely unreal to me. Of course, advances were paid by Sony on each album but only after it was completed and delivered to the record company. Given the deteriorating relationship between the record label and the singer I believe Sony paid the bills direct to the parties involved (recording studio, musicians, producers, etc.) and charged it to Jackson's royalty account. Either that or a separate accounting arrangement was set up.

As for the $25 million spent on promotion, yes, it is there in the accounts under marketing expenditure. In fact the amount is slightly higher than the reported $25 million. The outlay is claimed to have reached $27.5 million. But as Taraborrelli noticed, there is no way of knowing how much was spent on effective promotion as opposed to expense-account entertainment. In addition, it doesn't matter how much money is thrown at a product if the campaign is incompetent, whether deliberate or not.

However, the larger the amount stated in the accounts, the more the record company can claw back out of the artist's royalties.

Taraborrelli then makes the most extraordinary statement, saying, 'He (Michael Jackson) had thought that the license to the masters (the mechanical copyright) of his biggest selling albums ... were to revert back to him in 2000 and (he) was counting the days until that would happen.' Taraborrelli goes on to say that once Jackson's advisors checked the contract 'they found that the classics revert back to Michael only if he releases about one new CD for Sony every couple of years – which was never going to happen.' It sounds to me as if someone with an agenda told Taraborrelli this story. It contains enough truth to have been revealed by a player with inside knowledge but the reality has been distorted and there are some additions which are surely inventions by Taraborrelli's source.

The assertion that Michael Jackson 'thought' the mechanical copyright would revert to him in 2000 is a reference to the Dunkirk Clause. But the Dunkirk Clause is not predicated on the provision of further albums. Rather, any requirement for more albums could only be invoked as one of a number of options available to the record label if the artist had not completely fulfilled the contractual obligations regarding the minimum number of albums and songs. Let's face it, in some cases when the Dunkirk Clause is activated, the record label might not want any more albums. This is usually because the label no longer believes the artist will sell. That subjective judgment cannot be used to nullify Dunkirk, so in that event, another formula applied, usually in the form of a cash adjustment or a gradually reducing ownership share on the part of the record company, rather than one cut-off point. This means that the copyright could have reverted to Jackson, but only if he fulfilled his part of the contract. Now either Jackson was not told this at the time or he was told and someone is twisting the facts. To me, it is inconceivable that Jackson did not know because that would mean he didn't realise, when he signed the contract, how many albums he would have to produce. That just doesn't happen, folks. No matter how ignorant an artist may be, there are two things he will be acutely aware of: he knows how much advance he is getting and how many albums the deal covers. And Michael Jackson is not ignorant.

Taraborrelli's use of the word 'thought' is interesting. For someone as experienced as Taraborrelli to tell us that Michael Jackson 'thought' something, it must have been Michael Jackson himself who told him or someone who, in the author's opinion, could be relied upon to know what the artist 'thought', in which case it must be an individual close to the star. The self-serving nature of the story tells me it must, at the very least, have been authorised by Jackson.

The rest of this section of Taraborrelli's book swings from certitude to sketchy in equal measure. So the date when Jackson 'thought' he would gain the copyrights is definite, the year 2000. But the albums he would be required to deliver are 'about one' every 'couple of years', which appears hazy to me. Are we expected to believe that after discovering he would not gain his copyrights in 2000, Jackson still didn't bother to find out the details of the situation? There is more. While Dunkirk could be invoked in 2000, that would mark the start of the process to agree how the clause would apply. The contract might well not have been due to expire until 2005 and although, in theory, it was possible for the process to be completed in a short time, in practice this cannot happen as Dunkirk is a complicated set of possibilities and options. The end result had to be agreed by the parties and it was likely to take some years.

But by 1998–9 Jackson's finances were in a mess and he needed a huge injection of cash. No wonder he was 'counting the days'. Jackson could never admit to having financial problems unless some other party could be blamed. The idea that poor, weird Michael Jackson was being screwed by Sony conveniently diverts attention from the real source of the singer's fiscal plight, himself. Michael Jackson was being screwed by Sony, but not like this.

The next bombshell from Taraborrelli's source really does exit Planet Reality. 'After some investigation into the matter (of the copyright reversion), it was learned that the same attorney who represented Michael on this deal (the overall contract) had also represented Sony.' Now Michael Jackson has employed some of the best lawyers in America in his time at the top. Numerous contracts have been negotiated on his behalf over the years. He knows the score. The assertion that his lawyer also represented Sony is absurd. When originally signed at the beginning of the 1990s, the contract was trumpeted, not least by Michael Jackson's spokespeople, as the 'billion dollar deal'. There were no complaints then. Even if there was only one lawyer (and to me that is one step away from impossible), whose fault would that be? It's not as if Jackson was some innocent, signing his first contract. He knew the rules concerning the hiring of lawyers and used them at every turn. He also kept tight control over the legal process. He was even prepared to employ the services of the odious Anthony Pellicano, a private detective whose questionable activities on behalf of his many celebrity clients over the years has led him to a jail cell. As far as the one-lawyer issue is concerned, had Sony known about any conflict of interest they would have put a stop to it immediately, since they would have been well aware of the consequences to their ability to enforce the contract.

I believe that what in fact happened can be traced ultimately to Tommy Mottola, via his eternal sidekick, a lawyer called Allen Grubman (whom Walter Yetnikoff dubbed 'The Grubber'). Mottola and Grubman came as a package, with Mottola the streetwise manager and Grubman his full time networker and negotiator. Actually, Grubman was first and foremost a music business attorney.

The entertainment industry is crammed with lawyers. Many of them do not formally practise law in the conventional sense but their skill in contracts and deal-making makes them an asset if they are on the level. Walter Yetnikoff, who became the best man in the business when dealing with artists, is a trained lawyer. So is Paul Russell. Those in their league tend to rise to positions of prominence in large record companies. Others stay notionally independent but it is often difficult to unravel some of their associations or work out whether they are acting in a legal capacity or not. Grubman fell into this category. Tommy Mottola had deployed Grubman to perform various tasks on his behalf for years. When Yetnikoff brought Mottola to CBS, Grubman, as always, was at his side.

For most of his time in the music business up to that point, Tommy Mottola had been a wheeler-dealer, a necessity for someone who does not have the salary and expense account a large corporation provides. During that time he became used to sending Allen Grubman to smooth his path, to oil the wheels. When Mottola became a company man, he continued the pattern that had served him so well. Soon the lines between who was acting for whom became blurred. At various times after Mottola joined Sony, Grubman found it necessary to have a word in Michael Jackson's ear. At around the time when Walter Yetnikoff was losing it and the new contract was being negotiated, Jackson fired his manager, Frank Delio, and his lawyer, John Branca. For a while, Jackson's confidant was unofficially Allen Grubman.

That, however, does not amount to Grubman representing both parties. Grubman's unconventional interpretation of any possible conflict of inerest would, though, have muddied the waters and, as Taraborrelli admits, have given Jackson some leverage in his ongoing arguments with Sony. Taraborrelli says the result of all this was that Michael Jackson 'managed to extricate himself from the entire Sony deal', although not until he delivered two more albums after 'Invincible'. One was to be a greatest hits package, which I think refers to the poor 'Number Ones', the other a box set. To date, no box set, to my knowledge, has seen the light of day, nor is any planned. It is an interesting way for Taraborrelli to put it but it bears only a passing resemblance to what really took place. Sony was in the process of dropping Jackson. Maybe Jackson wanted to go. But normally, when an artist of Jackson's stature leaves a label, it is because at least one other major company is waiting in the wings with an open cheque book. No such offer existed for Jackson.

Taraborrelli doesn't mention what happened to the ownership of the mechanical copyright to Jackson's back catalogue. It just seems to disappear from view as an issue. In fact, the final status of Jackson's relationship with Sony was still some way off as the star fought to save his finances while at the same time trying to record 'Invincible'.

The subtlety of Sony's approach is lost when you read Taraborrelli's account. The Japanese were not simply relying on the efforts of Tommy Mottola. To Taraborrelli, or his source, it was a simple case of Michael Jackson battling away with Sony. But why, then, did Sony step in to fill the breach in Jackson's finances by agreeing the series of loans Jackson took out with the Bank of America? The answer, as we now know, is that Sony was playing long. And those in charge wanted ownership, not just of Jackson's mechanical copyrights, but the even bigger prize of Sony ATV.

Even without *Living with Michael Jackson* Norio Ohga believed that eventually Jackson's borrowings would ovetake him. Then Sony could move. Suddenly, with the investigation by 'Mad Dog' Sneddon, and the passing to the DA of the financial information, everything was about to come to a head. It was now more crucial than ever that Sony's true role remained out of the prying eyes of the media and the public.

7

TRIAL AND ERROR

Tom Sneddon held a news conference on November 19, 2003. The months since the February screening of *Living with Michael Jackson* had been filled with conjecture, leaks and statements from everybody who was anybody and the rest. Neverland had been raided by an army of over two hundred and fifty of Santa Barbara's finest, heavy hints had been dropped to the effect that there were other victims apart from Gavin Arvizo, and the DA was aggressively telling anyone who listened that he had a 'strong case'. It was in this context that Sneddon announced to a large contingent of the media: 'Within a very short space of time, there will be charges filed against Mr Jackson.' Sneddon's tone at the news conference was at odds with the seriousness of what he was saying. He was triumphalist, cocky and over-confident. The DA was later forced to apologise for his attitude. Those who had seen him over the years were not fooled. As Jerry Roberts, editor of the Santa Barbara News-Press told CBS News correspondent, Hattie Kaufman, 'I think people do feel that he (Sneddon) is a man on a mission. You know this is going to be the signature case of his career.'

Roberts was proved right. When charges were filed against Jackson in December (just before Christmas), Sneddon had already decided to try the case himself. If Sneddon's intention really was justice, his ego-fuelled decision was a grave mistake. He could not supply the necessary detachment to convince the jury of his credibility. If Sneddon was only interested in personal publicity, it was a coup. He was Santa Barbara's longest serving DA and wasn't going to stand for the office again. He couldn't lose, even if he lost. In that event someone else would have to carry the can. The possibility of losing, however, did not enter his mind. The rematch was arranged. Now all he had to do was win.

As I watched the pictures of the media circus gathered around the courthouse in Santa Maria, I was reminded of the scenes at the Oxford

Union when OJ Simpson appeared there. Like Simpson's, the trial of Michael Jackson was being followed, commented upon and analysed by news organisations the world over and they all seemed to have representatives in the town. There was also a large number of Jackson's fans, who had come from all corners of the planet to support their idol. Some had even given up their jobs and left their families to be in Santa Maria for the duration. Judge Melville, in light of the effect in the Simpson case, refused to allow the trial to be televised. That did not deter the world's more ferocious news-gatherers. Some, such as Sky News in Europe, produced dramatised versions of each day's proceedings. They were highly selective, however, so we were dependant on the judgment of the editors to give us an accurate and balanced account of what was going on. And as we have seen, that is not something on which you'd want to bet your mortgage.

So concerned were the pundits with the details as they unfolded, and such was the prejudice towards acceptance of the claims of the prosecution, they failed completely to spot what, for me, was the fulcrum on which the outcome of the trial turned. Tom Sneddon was obsessed with nailing his adversary. But his adversary in court was not the object of his obsession, Michael Jackson. It was Tom Mesereau. Mesereau, who helped defend the actor, Robert Blake (*In Cold Blood, Baretta*), on charges of murdering his wife, took over Jackson's defence after the singer fired his attorney, Mark Geragos. Jackson hardly uttered a word throughout the hearings. No doubt Sneddon had rehearsed how he would cross-examine the star but Jackson never gave evidence, as is his right. Tom Sneddon's own demons were about to catch up with him. He was, it has to be said, no match for Mesereau, perhaps because he was fighting Jackson, not the star's attorney. The distortion in Sneddon's focus that his mistake caused left him unable to see the holes in his case and ultimately, in my view, reduced his effectiveness with the jury.

The area where Michael Jackson did take Sneddon on was in the realm of public relations. This is Jackson's natural territory and he wiped the floor with the DA, who couldn't help but come across as sanctimonious, smug and ever-so-slightly unstable. Even when Jackson did something outrageous, like standing on the roof of his car to entertain the crowd after one of the preliminary hearings, it worked in his favour, invoking first incredulity, then confirmation of our belief that Michael Jackson – aka Jacko – is, well, weird. And who can forget the time he arrived in court in his pyjamas after the drama of the bad back and the visit to the emergency room? Jackson also managed, through Mesereau, to get permission from Judge Melville to make a statement protesting his innocence on video which was broadcast to the nation and the world on the eve of the trial. That was followed by his appearance on Jesse Jackson's radio show. Tom Sneddon stood no chance.

Nevertheless, Jackson still faced severe problems. Foremost among them was the nature of the charges he faced. Evidence can always be contested but in the Jackson case, Tom Sneddon paid great – I would say too much – attention to the number of charges on the indictment. First of all, there were so many of them. Each count of committing a lewd act had a lesser counter-part, so the jury, if they felt the more serious allegations were not proved, could still find the star guilty on the lesser charges. By doing this, Sneddon gave himself two bites of the cherry on each alleged criminal action. Then there were the alcohol charges. If the words 'supplying alcohol to a minor in furtherance of a felony' are used then that is a serious charge. The lesser charge leaves out the 'in furtherance of a felony' part. Therefore, the jury only had to believe that Jackson gave a sip of an alcoholic drink to one of the Arvizo children and he was guilty. Innocent intent is no defence.

I have offered my own children a glass of wine with a meal since they were ten years-old. In Europe this happens all the time. If I had done this in California would I have been committing a criminal offence? I guess I would. If all else failed, it was an easy option for the jury to find Jackson guilty of supplying alcohol to a minor. Were he to be convicted on even one of those counts, Jackson might well have been given serious jail time.

Finally, and most importantly, there was the conspiracy charge. Conspiracy occupies an odd position in the legal system in that it does not require what would normally be regarded as a criminal act to have taken place. If two or more people discuss or plan anything criminal, they can be guilty of conspiracy to commit a criminal act whether or not the crime is ever carried out. On occasion, bringing a charge of conspiracy might well be justified (such as when it prevents a crime taking place) but it is often used as a lazy option by prosecutors who do not really possess enough evidence to secure a conviction for the criminal act itself. Conspiracy can be difficult to prove for the same reason it can be difficult to defend. In the absence of surveillance evidence, what might have been said or written is always open to differences of recall and interpretation. However, it can carry a penalty as great as would be handed down if convicted of the actual crime itself.

In the Jackson case, the charge of conspiracy was laid after the alleged events to which it related took place, so it was not used to prevent a crime. The evidence Sneddon possessed was mainly in the form of statements by members of the Arvizo family. But if the things the Arvizos claimed occurred, did occur, why were no charges brought for the acts themselves, rather than conspiracy to commit the acts? In the answer to that question lies the true motive of Tom Sneddon.

The supposed imprisonment, harassment and coercion of the Arvizo family were not carried out by Michael Jackson personally. To charge Jackson in connection with these crimes, it was necessary for Sneddon to prove that he ordered or consented to the felonious behaviour and discussed its details with those who carried it out. At the very least the prosecution would have to show some chain of command which could link Jackson to the perpetrators, even if indirectly. According to the Arvizos their imprisonment was executed by people employed by the singer, who orchestrated the whole business. One of the prosecution's witnesses, Jay Jackson, who is Janet Arvizo's new husband (so her name is now Janet Jackson), said that Mrs Arvizo, after being held captive at Neverland, went to stay at his home in Los Angeles with her children. While she was there she received numerous phone calls from one of Jackson's aides, one Frank Tyson. These calls, Jay Jackson continued, caused great distress. 'She was emotional, she was crying. She was sitting in the closet having these conversations with Frank.' Jay Jackson, however, shed no light on what the contents of these conversations might have been so his evidence was really tangential.

However, if we take the implications of this testimony at face value, justice would suggest that Tyson and other individuals responsible for this type of reprehensible behaviour be arrested and charged with any crimes committed. If evidence emerged pointing to the involvement of anyone else, including Michael Jackson, they could be charged too, perhaps at that point with conspiracy. But Sneddon's aim was not to achieve justice in the way most of us understand the word's meaning. His objective was to get Michael Jackson. Nothing could be allowed to divert him from that goal. Arresting lots of Jackson's associates was not on Sneddon's agenda. However, the prosecutor needed to be able to introduce evidence of the details of the conspiracy for the jury to make sense of Sneddon's version of events. Defending the conspiracy allegation would also divert effort and resources on the part of the defence team. Michael Jackson thus found himself in the unusual position of being the only person charged with engaging in the conspiracy, even though the identities of those with whom he supposedly conspired were known to the prosecuting authorities.

Fortunately for Jackson, Tom Mesereau realised the game Sneddon was playing. If the evidence of the commission of a crime is strong a prosecutor will more often than not stick to one, or at the most two, main charges. It keeps things simple for the jury and ensures the focus of the trial remains within narrow boundaries. When a plethora of charges is brought over a single alleged crime, the less likely it is that the prosecution is certain of its case. I admit this is a generalisation but it nonetheless holds good in the Jackson case. Mesereau's response to Sneddon's strategy of multiple charges was to challenge everything, however insignificant. No matter what any given prosecution witness said, their evidence would not be allowed to pass without Mesereau launching an attack on their credibility, motives and truthfulness. It would be a massive work-load but it was the only way to expose what must – so Mesereau's thinking went – be a thin case indeed if so many scattergun charges were in the indictment.

One of Sneddon's first ploys when the trial got under way was to send his deputy, Gordon Auchincloss, to argue before the judge that the prosecution should be granted access to Michael Jackson's financial records. They needed the information, Auchincloss explained, to show that the state of Jackson's finances was so bad it caused him to panic after *Living with Michael Jackson* was broadcast. Auchincloss' argument was that the singer feared a public backlash so he imprisoned, threatened and coerced the Arvizos into making a video rebutting all the inferences contained in Martin Bashir's programme. 'We believe,' Auchincloss continued, 'Mr Jackson is on the precipice of bankruptcy'. Auchincloss did not disclose – perhaps he was not aware of – the source of his information. Whether it might have made a difference to the judge's decision, we cannot know but if Judge Melville had found for the defence on this application, Tom Sneddon would have had to rethink his whole strategy. One of Jackson's defence attorneys, Robert Sanger, answered on behalf of the star, saying, 'Mr Jackson's assets are worth more than prosecutors estimated.' He did, though, go as far as to admit that 'liquidity from time to time may be a problem.'

Chapter 7

Some ten years before the trial in Santa Maria, a California judge had allowed Tom Sneddon to examine Michael Jackson's body. Now, Judge Melville gave Sneddon access to Jackson's finances. Two of the things which are most personal and intimate had been grossly violated, to no useful effect in my view. The prosecution engaged a forensic accountant, John Duross O'Bryan, to look at the singer's assets and liabilities. Having already received the so-called facts he needed from Sony, the DA would now be able to get the information into evidence through the forensic accountant. There was no way anyone from Sony was going testify as to Jackson's financial position (or anything else for that matter) but if O'Bryan was pointed in the right direction he could put meat on the bare bones of the prosecutors' knowledge.

I believe the effectiveness of O'Bryan's testimony to the court failed to match the aspirations of Tom Sneddon. First, Tom Mesereau fiercely objected to O'Bryan giving evidence at all. The accountant's conclusions, Mesereau maintained, were hearsay based on a few memos from some of Jackson's financial advisors. Not only that, it was irrelevant to the case. Judge Melville did not agree and O'Bryan was called to the stand. His analysis, however, seemed to me simplistic and superficial. He told the court that he had tracked Jackson's finances between 1999 and 2004. It is interesting to note these two dates. The so-called 'forensic' accounting began in 1999, the year when Jackson first began borrowing from the Bank of America, thus it covered a period when Jackson's financial situation was at its worst. We either have to accept that the two dates are the same by coincidence or that they were deliberately chosen on the basis of the information from Sony.

O'Bryan told the court that he had only seen one balance sheet relating to Jackson's finances. It dated from 2002 and had shown the singer to be in debt to the tune of $285 million. Once again, the date of 2002 fits the Sony information exactly as it covers all the various loans Jackson took out against his shares in Sony ATV. The final loan was made in 2003. Could that be another coincidence? The 2002 balance sheet would have covered the initial tranche of loans carried forward. The cut-off at 2004 ensured that all the borrowings and interest charges were included.

When he cross-examined the witness, Mesereau suggested that O'Bryan had underestimated the value of Jackson's assets. O'Bryan then gave what he and the prosecution thought would be the killer fact for the jury. In

February 2003, when *Living with Michael Jackson* was shown, 'Mr Jackson had unpaid invoices totalling $10.5 million but had only $38,000 cash in his bank accounts,' O'Bryan said. However, the idea that Michael Jackson, creator of 'Thriller', only possessed $38,000 was too much for the jury to swallow. When O'Bryan was finished in the witness stand the impression he left behind was one of incredulity, not the expert analysis for which Sneddon had prepared.

I asked Paul Russell about O'Bryan's evidence. He was contemptuous of the forensic accountant's work. 'Michael Jackson, Paul said, 'Is sometimes cash-poor, but he is asset-rich and he is not close to going broke. It just ain't gonna happen guys.' In the year or so since the trial finished, Michael Jackson has suffered further financial reverses. He has not, however, been made bankrupt. If he could survive when he had to fight a court case and with his career flat-lining, then surely Tom Sneddon was wrong when he had Gordon Auchincloss declare that Jackson was 'on the precipice of bankruptcy.'

The problem for Sneddon was that if the jury did not accept his 'close to broke' story, then the rest of his case fell as it was all based on this one premise. Jackson needed money desperately, that's why he hooked up with Martin Bashir. When that went wrong the magnitude of his financial problems sent Jackson into a manic spin. He therefore organised the coercion to hold the Arvizos captive and force them to participate in a video denying any wrongdoing on Jackson's part. While he was doing this he plied the youngsters with alcohol and sexually abused Gavin Arvizo. This was the chain of events the prosecution was putting forward. But if there was no financial desperation, then none of the subsequent events could have taken place as described.

If John Duross O'Bryan failed to deliver the knockout blow, other prosecution witnesses fared even worse, at least as far as Tom Sneddon was concerned. Having started with Martin Bashir, Sneddon's final witness was someone he believed would end his case with a bang. It was Debbie Rowe, the mother of Jackson's two children and the singer's ex-wife. Sneddon, knowing that Rowe and Jackson had not always been the happy couple, believed Rowe would attack Jackson on the stand. Sneddon expected her to label Jackson a sociopath, as she was said to have done previously. However, Rowe was a disaster for Sneddon and as she was his last witness, it was difficult for him to recover his position. 'We've been friends and we were married,' Rowe told the court. She went on to say that the pair had known each other for over twenty years before they married. Then she dropped her bombshell. She praised Jackson as a parent and said any problems in his life were caused by the hangers-on surrounding the singer. 'Vultures' she called them. This was believed to be a reference to at least two former managers of Michael Jackson, Ronald Konitzer and Dieter Wiesner, who, according to a lawyer, David LeGrand, diverted over $1million of Jackson's money for their own purposes. This was not what Tom Sneddon had been expecting at all.

I spoke to three lawyers not long after the trial began. All said they believed Jackson's guilt or innocence would hang on the performance in court of Janet Arvizo, mother of Jackson's accuser, Gavin. This was because she was the main adult witness to the conspiracy charge and because, whatever her children said, her decision to allow her young son to share a bedroom with Michael Jackson needed explaining. Tom Mesereau claimed all along that the whole case was a scam to obtain a large sum of money from Michael Jackson. The architect of the scam, according to Mesereau, was Janet Arvizo, who coached her children to lie as part of her plan.

Just as he had used Anthony Pellicano in the Chandler case, so Jackson, through Mesereau, turned to a private investigator to dig up some dirt on Janet Arvizo. This time the detective was Scott Ross, who had, like Mesereau, helped the actor, Robert Blake, by finding negative lifestyle information on Blake's dead wife, Bonnie Lee Backley. Many believe that Ross' smears gave the jury a reason to dislike her. Ross later told the Los Angeles Times that Mesereau asked him to 'do to her (Janet Arvizo) what you did to Bonnie Lee Backley'. Ross also exposed unlawful behaviour on the part of Arvizo, namely welfare fraud stemming from not declaring money she received from a court case settlement. Ross also claimed that Janet Arvizo lied in her testimony to the court in the same litigation. When Mrs Arvizo did testify in Michael Jackson's trial, Sneddon's case went from bad to worse.

Janet Arvizo's testimony was best summed up by Laurie Leveson, a professor at Loyola Law School in Los Angeles, who said, 'It was a bizarre charge and now it's a bizarre charge supported by a bizarre witness.' Janet Arvizo referred to Jackson and his staff as 'killers'. She constantly pointed to Jackson and spoke directly to the singer from the witness box. She would click her fingers and stare at the defendant and the jurors. One moment she was in floods of tears, the next she made a wisecrack. She rarely answered a question without a rambling exposition into areas no one could understand. She seemed overly fixated on an accusation that Jackson's people had faked a receipt for services provided by a beauty parlour. The receipt said she had undergone a leg, eyebrow and bikini wax. 'It was only a leg wax', she kept repeating. And this was before she was cross-examined. When it came to his turn, Mesereau was at his scathing best. His questions led to Mrs. Arvizo admitting she had lied in a previous compensation case. 'I'm a bad actress,' she said. Immediately, Mesereau retorted with the comment, 'I think you're a very good actress'. She refused point blank to answer other questions regarding her financial probity. To those enquiries, she pleaded the fifth amendment, a constitutional right which says a witness does not have to answer a question if the truthful response would incriminate them. Jackson's attorney asked why, if she had been held prisoner as she claimed, she never once called the police or anyone else, 'I was hoping it would all go away, I was afraid of him (Jackson). Who could possibly believe this?' she replied.

The most damning thing she said was that 'Neverland is all about booze, pornography and sex with boys'. Once again, the media latched onto this dramatic statement as evidence against Jackson. The trouble was, the jury could well think that if this was indeed the case, what on earth was she doing letting her children (and herself) spend so much time there?

Tom Sneddon did not conduct the examination of Janet Arvizo himself. It was, instead, left to one of his assistants, Ron Zonen. The trial was supposed to be Sneddon's defining case but he didn't personally examine his most important witness in court. Perhaps he and Arvizo just didn't gel. Or perhaps Sneddon had a sneaking feeling that she might end up being more helpful to the defence than the prosecution. In that case, by leaving Janet Arvizo to Ron Zonen, if anything went wrong, it wouldn't be Sneddon's fault. And it did go wrong. Zonen, despite several attempts, failed to get Arvizo to establish any direct connection between the alleged conspiracy and Michael Jackson.

As for the Arvizo children, they were on a hiding to nothing. They had made statements denying that Michael Jackson had abused them. It was hardly a surprise when Mesereau tied them up in knots for changing their stories. The unfortunate Gavin, a cancer sufferer whose recovery from the disease was surely put in jeopardy by his ordeal, could not dispel Mesereau's assertion that the boy was either bad or being controlled by his mother and the prosecution.

Gavin said in court that Michael Jackson had given him wine to drink, which the singer called 'Jesus juice' (presumably, although this was never mentioned, because Jesus is said to have turned water into wine at a wedding feast). Gavin also accused Jackson of showing him pornography and sexually assaulting him. But Gavin, as well as his brother and sister, made mistakes in their testimonies which called into question either their truthfulness or the accuracy of their recollections of events.

Sneddon had for some time been busy describing Jackson as a classic paedophile, one who groomed, then sexually abused boys, generally those with family problems and absent fathers. In his closing statement, Ron Zonen called it 'the world of the forbidden'. He also said that Neverland was a 'no rules, no manners environment,' designed for the purposes of abuse. But if any of this were true, where were the other victims and why wasn't Jackson charged in connection with them? Sneddon was helped by child abuse experts, who claimed in their numerous media appearances they knew how serial paedophiles behaved and accused Jackson of just such behaviour. They also accounted for Gavin's earlier denials of abuse – he said he 'didn't want to be made fun of at school' – by saying they were examples of classic victim behaviour. This means youngsters are telling the truth if they admit they have been abused but lying if they deny it.

Since Sneddon had no other victims, despite his earlier public calls for more to come forward if they had a complaint against Jackson, he tried another tack. He asked Judge Melville to allow evidence of prior (similar) behaviour on Jackson's part. This was a coded method of deciding to dredge up the Jordan Chandler affair. This time, Sneddon argued the prosecution's case himself. He declared that he wanted to 'present evidence relating to five previous accusers, aged ten to thirteen, two of whom had settled out of court with Mr Jackson.' Furthermore, Sneddon claimed the evidence would show a pattern 'very similar, if not identical' to the abuse in the Arvizo allegations. That sounds pretty impressive but closer examination revealed it was not all it seemed. For instance, if the accusers' stories were true, why hadn't Jackson been charged with any of the crimes they alleged he committed. The two cases where a settlement was agreed after money changed hands may have occurred before the law was changed but what about the other three? Then Sneddon admitted that only one of the actual accusers would be appearing. He wanted the judge to allow nine 'third parties' who had knowledge of these 'prior acts of abuse' to testify.

For centuries, prior act evidence has been avoided in the American system and its antecedent, English Law, because it is not evidence relevant to the crime with which the defendant is charged. Moreover, it has a prejudicial effect over and above any probative value. This principle has been breached in recent years, particularly in cases of a sexual nature such as rape or child abuse. Despite Mesereau's response that the prosecution was trying desperate measures after their case had unravelled, Judge Melville allowed the prior acts testimony. Mesereau was beside himself. Letting the testimony in would, he said, 'reduce the burden of proof and the presumption of innocence.' However, Judge Melville, in his ruling, said 'I'm going to permit testimony with regard to sexual offences and alleged pattern of grooming activity by the defendant.'

Michael Jackson, when he appeared on the Jesse Jackson radio show, protested his innocence of any prior acts of grooming or abuse. 'None of these stories are true,' he said. 'They are totally fabricated'.

What seemed like a miracle for the prosecution actually did them no favours. One of the alleged 'victims' was the actor and star of the 'Home Alone' movies, McCauley Culkin. But Culkin himself did not appear for the prosecution. Indeed he claimed on many occasions that he suffered no abuse at Jackson's hands. The main witness was an ex-maid of Jackson's who said she observed inappropriate actions by Jackson with Culkin in the 1990s. She also claimed to have seen similar goings-on between Jackson and Jordan Chandler. One of Jackson's former security guards, Ralph Chacon, claimed to have seen Jackson performing oral sex on Chandler. Chacon, who had lost a law-suit against Michael Jackson which left the security man penniless, saw his credibility torn asunder as this information was revealed to the jury by Mesereau.

A further ex-maid, Bianca Francia, said she saw Jackson with another alleged victim, Wade Robson. Her son, Jason, aged 24 at the time of the trial, was the only alleged victim to testify. He claimed Jackson had masturbated him as a child. Mesereau asked him about $2.4 million collected from Jackson when he originally made the allegation. He admitted taking the money. There was also some incidental evidence concerning another boy, an Australian called Brett Barnes, but that was inconclusive.

As for the most well-known of Jackson's accusers, Jordan Chandler, he did not appear at all. Chandler has hidden himself away in the years since the settlement with Jackson. Instead, Sneddon called Chandler's mother, June, from whom Chandler is so estranged they have had no contact since the events of the mid-nineties.

June Chandler recounted the story of how Jackson reacted when she questioned the propriety of the singer sleeping in the same bed as her young son. The confrontation took place in Las Vegas in 1993. 'He (Jackson) was sobbing and crying and shaking and trembling,' she said. She then claimed Jackson pleaded with her to allow him to sleep with Jordan, saying, 'You don't trust me, we are family, why are you doing this to me?' After 'twenty or thirty or forty minutes of this', June Chandler relented and told Jackson that Jordan could visit his bedroom. The idea that a mother of a pre-adolescent child would consent to him visiting the bedroom of a man in his thirties beggared belief.

Another Jackson aide, Bob Jones, was called to repeat what he had written in an unpublished book, which alleged Jackson had indulged himself by licking Jordan Chandler's head. However, when asked if he had himself seen Jackson licking Jordan's head, he replied, 'No sir'. When pressed, Jones went further, saying 'I don't recall ever seeing any head-licking,' Another Jackson employee who had told prosecutors he brought wine to the singer and a number of under-age boys, changed his story on the stand and said he may well have brought fizzy soft drinks as well. The air stewardesses who were supposed to have delivered alcohol to the Arvizo children on air flights actually said at the trial that they only remembered giving wine to Jackson.

To any rational observer, Sneddon's case was falling apart. That was not how he saw it, however. The prosecution team believed they were on course for a conviction. They were egged on by large sections of the American media, who seemed not to have learned any lessons from the OJ Simpson trial. By the time Sneddon brought the prosecution case to an end, many US pundits had already convicted the King of Pop in the court of public opinion.

In his opening speech, Tom Meseareau claimed a roll-call of over 350 witnesses who would be appearing for Jackson. It was a who's who of Planet Celebrity. There would be Elizabeth Taylor, Diana Ross, Stevie Wonder, Barry Gibb, Kobe Bryant (star basketball player for the LA

Lakers, who himself was having legal difficulties, and was being sued by a woman in Colorado who said Bryant attacked her sexually in 2003), and ten members of Jackson's family. Mesereau also dropped a heavy hint that Jackson himself would testify. 'Michael Jackson will tell you ...' was how Mesereau put it. In the event, most of the celebrities did not appear. One, Larry King, was rejected as a witness by the judge and another, Jay Leno, added nothing to the discourse. Jackson, as we all now know, did not give evidence. I believe Mesereau never intended to put Jackson on the stand unless absolutely necessary. Mesereau's reading of the case told him that not only was it not necessary, it wasn't even a close call. Getting Jackson to give evidence would expose him to many days of harsh cross-examination by Tom Sneddon. Mesereau saw his job as keeping Jackson out of the firing line.

The star whose appearance did make a difference was the actor who did not appear for the prosecution when Sneddon introduced the 'prior acts' testimony, McCauley Culkin He was one of the youngsters Sneddon said Jackson had abused in the past. He was called by the defence. 'He never molested me,' Culkin revealed, 'I think I'd realise if something like that had happened.' This was a severe setback to the prosecution since if a so-called victim said it never happened, surely all the other 'prior acts' evidence was suspect. Sneddon needed to show Culkin was either a liar or mistaken. Strangely, he once again abdicated his responsibility when the going got tough and left Culkin's cross-examination to the ever-willing Ron Zonen.

According to Dan Glaister, who reported on the trial for The Guardian, a London newspaper, Zonen subjected Culkin to some 'bruising questioning.' Culkin, however, 'held his ground, insisting that his friendship with Mr Jackson had been borne of a shared history, rather than any desire by the singer to groom him, as the prosecutors allege.' Culkin was also asked what he thought of the charges for which Jackson was being tried. 'I think they are absolutely ridiculous,' he said. The best the prosecution could come up with in the face of Culkin's broadside was to suggest that they had attempted to talk to Culkin but the actor had refused to speak with them. It was pretty threadbare stuff.

Mesereau believed the prosecution case was holed below the waterline. He saw no need to call Michael Jackson. Mesereau's final witness was the actor and comedian, Chris Tucker. Tucker said he had befriended the Arvizo family and helped them financially, on one occasion giving them $1500. Then, Tucker said, he began to have reservations: 'I started getting nervous. She (Janet Arvizo) started crying, not in the normal way. She started acting, like, frantically, like, mentally. Something wasn't right.' One strand of Tom Sneddon's narrative was that Michael Jackson tried to prevent the Arvizos from watching the broadcast of *Living with Michael Jackson* by having them flown off to Miami, where he would meet them. In other words, Jackson was manipulating the Arvizos' movements as a prelude to the kidnapping and false imprisonment – the conspiracy. Chris Tucker, however, had accompanied the Arvizos on the Miami trip and reported to the court that they were desperate to be with Jackson. 'Janet Arvizo', said Tucker, 'was frantically saying, "Michael is the father"'. When Jackson arrived Tucker took him to another room and said: 'Something ain't right.' In a sideswipe at Gavin, Tucker described the boy as 'smart, cunning at times but I always overlooked it.'

It may seem that I have concentrated on the deficiencies in the prosecution case and given the defence's arguments an easier ride. But it is the prosecution's job to prove the worth of its allegations. A defendant does not have to prove anything. Therefore, if, as it appears to me to have been the situation in the Michael Jackson trial, the Santa Barbara District Attorney presented a case as full of holes as occurred in the courtroom in Santa Maria, then whatever the defence asserts is, in some ways, irrelevant. And let's not mince words here. The evidence Tom Sneddon relied on, and his interpretation of the chain of events, was appalling. In my opinion, part of the responsibility for the trial going as far as it did in part lay with Judge Melville, who allowed so much latitude to the prosecution that the trial, and the media coverage of it, became distorted in the extreme.

This meant that as the trial approached its climax, with Michael Jackson fighting for his life, even more 'vultures' were gathering than Debbie Rowe could have realised.

8

THE AMERICANS FIGHT BACK

When Michael Jackson was arrested, no one was more appalled at the turn of events than the officers of the Bank of America. The bank is one of America's most 'establishment' institutions. It was one of the first US banks to become a national business. Traditionally, American banks were based in the state in which they began their operations, or in some cases, the smaller unit of the county. Until the 1980s, for instance, it was difficult to get most of them to change foreign currency. That the bank was nervous is not surprising. Jackson, after all, was into them for a considerable amount of money. They held security in the form of Jackson's shares in Sony ATV and Mijack, but once the child-abuse charges had been laid, anything could happen. The first thing the bank wanted to do was keep its role in Jackson's finances secret. The second was to offload the debt as soon as possible.

Soon after the Paul Russell article appeared in the *Mail on Sunday*, the Bank of America, with a huge sigh of relief, managed to transfer Jackson's mortgage to a New York investment group called Fortress, which specialises in high-risk debts. Fortress is often referred to as a hedge fund, although it has broadened its activities in recent years. The timing of the sequence of events which occurred over this period is instructive. As Jackson's trial got underway, both Sony and the Bank of America were increasingly concerned about the possible effect the circus would have on their respective operations. The Bank of America was looking to get rid of Jackson's debt. Negotiations soon opened with Fortress. All this occurred in secret. Then Paul Russell and I unwittingly threw a huge spanner in the works with the *Mail on Sunday* report. Almost immediately, Sony's lawyers attempted to silence Paul Russell. Could it be that the deal with Fortress was put in jeopardy by Russell's revelations? Sony did not want to assume Jackson's debt but they needed to ensure that any disposal by the Bank of America went smoothly. The situation was no longer secret. But perhaps not everything had yet come out.

The Lennon and McCartney catalogue was now passing into the hands of a Japanese corporation and Wall Street speculators. It must almost have made Paul McCartney nostalgic for Sir Lew Grade. Meanwhile, the erstwhile saviour and self-appointed custodian of pop music's greatest songs would be required to keep up a schedule of massive interest payments if he were not to lose his main asset.

Hedge funds like Fortress are a relatively new phenomenon in the financial markets. Their time came when the twenty-year US bull market came to an end in 2000. While investors took a fall in the value of their equity holdings, some fund managers were placing 'bets' on stocks going down. In a poorly performing stock market, many of them made fortunes. These funds also used the leverage they acquired through options and derivatives trading to boost their spectacular results further. Financial journalist, Aaron Pressman, takes up the story. 'With low barriers to entry (between 2000 and 2002),' he said, 'New hedge funds sprouted every-where, from the marbled corridors of Wall Street to the home offices of day traders'.

Profits were huge as long as the hedge funds outperformed the stock market. After 2002, as the market recovered, this became far more difficult, so other avenues were sought out. Traditionally, transactions like borrowing were predicated on what would now be called good credit ratings. Some of those running hedge funds, however, are as creative as any artist. They realised there could be profits in bad debt, just as there had been in the decline in the price of stock. The fund managers began to speculate on high-risk ventures. In the case of loans, a fund would make money first by charging hefty debt-management fees and second through interest charges. If a speculation went well, then further profits would accrue. Typically, a hedge fund charges one or two per cent of the value of the assets it manages and up to fifty per cent of any profit. Moreover, investors' cash is tied up for as long as a year.

As the stock market recovered after 2002, hedge funds lost some of their lustre. One of them, the Bayou Group, which looked after funds totalling $450 million, was embroiled in a fraud case. It was closed down in 2005 after two of its leaders pleaded guilty to deception. Other hedge funds also failed as the going got tough and many predicted the imminent demise of the whole sector. For example, the Executive Director of the Commonfund Institute, which provides advice to investors, John

Griswold, said: 'The really smart money is wary of getting into hedge funds now.' Despite this, hedge funds account for over $1,100 billion of assets. And in May 2006 a survey by *Alpha*, a magazine for institutional investors, showed that the top twenty-six hedge fund managers had 'pocketed an average of $300 million each in 2005.' The biggest earner was James Simons of Renaissance Technologies, who made a cool $1.2 billion. In the past, hedge funds tended to keep a low profile outside the financial press. With Fortress's very public acquisition of the Bank of America's loans to Michael Jackson, however, hedge funds became trendsetters again, paving the way towards a new future where even the insolvent could join the rest of society and borrow, borrow, borrow. It reminded me of a joke advertisement I once saw in an American satirical magazine: 'Get out of debt, free,' it read.

In perhaps the most bizarre episode in the history of the finance industry, hedge fund managers gathered, in June 2006, for what was laughingly called a trade fair. It took place at Knebworth House in rural southern England, the scene of many a famous rock festival in the past. Organised along the lines of Woodstock, the event, was called 'Headstock' and drew a crowd of four thousand hard-core hedge fund workers and investors. Along with combos put together by amateur musicians among the hedge fund people, Headstock managed to give the gathering a storming climax by organising an appearance by The Who, who appeared at the strange festival in return for donations to their favourite charities.

In Tokyo, the sale to Fortress was greeted with something approaching euphoria. It was excellent news. They just had to wait for Michael Jackson to default on his interest payments, which was bound to happen sooner or later. Then they could move. The numbers, which of course Sony controlled, said so. Norio Ohga's task was to hand on to the next generation what had been built out of the rubble of war: a world-wide corporation which itself was almost an imperial society within the wider society; a corporate culture which bound together all who embraced it; and, perhaps most important of all, the contribution Sony made and would continue to make to the new Japan. The rest is transient. Nothing could be allowed to interfere with the majesty of the Band of Brothers' creation. This was Norio Ohga's sacred duty.

But what was the true state of the corporation Ohga handed on as he slowly moved into the background? The story of Sony consists of a smooth progression from humble beginnings to global superpower. At least that's what the corporation would like us to believe. It is true that the list of technological achievements is impressive, from transistors to the DVD. There was one great blip, of course, the famous video wars of the 1970s and 80s, when Sony's expensively developed Betamax system was defeated by its rival, VHS.

The first in-depth analysis I heard concerning the video wars came from Gerald O'Connell in the early 1980s. O'Connell, a philosophy graduate of Cambridge University who is severely under-recognised for his contribution to the spread of sports broadcasting on satellite television in Europe, understood before anyone else that Sony's failure said something far more significant than normally applies to trade wars. O'Connell, along with accountant Mark Rooney, invented the application of premium rate telephone calls to football clubs, in the process creating the original and wildly successful Clubcall operation. The company which made the money out of O'Connell's idea was British Telecom (BT). BT funded Clubcall and subsequently sold it the Ladbrokes betting empire for $75million. Even the football clubs lost out in the initial years of Clubcall because they never believed their fans would stump up money each week for news about their clubs. How times change. These days, football clubs manage to squeeze every last penny out of their supporters (Michael Jackson had an interest in soccer. Through the famous psychic, Uri Geller, Jackson got involved for a short time in the affairs of Exeter City, a lowly club in the English West Country of which Geller was a director).

Gerald O'Connell went on to provide the marketing raison-d'etre for a subscription sports channel broadcasting from a satellite platform way before Rupert Murdoch cornered the market. One day he put it to me like this:

'Lynton,' he asked, 'would you pay ten pounds ($13) a month to watch every match played by the team you support (in my case, Leicester City)?

'Yes,' came my instant reply,

'Even if the games weren't shown live but in a delayed time schedule?'

'Yes, of course I would.'

'Do you believe other fans would do the same?'

'I'm sure they would.'

At the time, the idea was revolutionary. In Britain today, at least three million homes pay to watch premium sports (mainly soccer) channels.

Unfortunately for O'Connell, the outfit which backed him in his idea was British Aerospace, revered as a blue chip company but one that at the time was paying more attention to its ill-advised acquisition of the doomed Rover motor car company than to its speculative adventure into the nascent satellite television service. It was not surprising that British Aerospace, which these days manufactures the Eurofighter jet and contributes to the passenger aircraft, the Airbus, was beaten to the punch by Sky.

O'Connell was one of the first to realise that Betamax would lose out to VHS because Sony made an assumption which turned out to be wrong. There was only a small difference but it was crucial. In fact, in the 1970s three separate and incompatible video systems were introduced. First onto the market was a European company, the Dutch electronics giant Philips. When Sony's Betamax and JVC's VHS appeared they were a slight improvement on the Philips product and thereafter Philips was always trying to catch up. Before too long, Philips was forced out of the game and it was left to the two Japanese corporations to slug it out for supremacy. One thing was for certain, the public did not like two systems.

There was general agreement that Sony's was the better technical system. The Betamax hardware was, however, more expensive than VHS. But the difference was not great enough to account for Betamax's failure. In those early days video tape recorders were expensive consumer items and the public was not averse to paying a bit more for the best system. The problem for Sony was that the company believed the main consumer usage would be based around off-air recording of television programmes. Consequently, pre-recorded video tapes such as movies were seen as secondary. In turn that meant that not enough attention was paid to the availability and price of software (pre-recorded tapes). The mistake cost Sony dear.

Meanwhile the VHS system, which could record off-air like Betamax, prioritised the creation of a catalogue of pre-recorded tapes. A whole new infrastructure was put in place to rent or sell them. Once the public got the idea that VHS offered more (and cheaper) titles, Betamax was finished. The Beta name survived in professional quality products for television studios but Sony was forced to throw in the towel and accept the victory of VHS for domestic machines. Sony swallowed its pride to the extent that it manufactured VHS video tape recorders itself.

The episode did not keep Sony down for long, however. The engineers and designers redoubled their efforts and progress was resumed as normal.

What really boosted Sony at this point were the incomparable Walkman and later, the CD and DVD. Before long, Sony was on a roll, completely recovered from the video wars fiasco and going from strength to strength. When the first Playstation hit the shops, it took Sony through the stratosphere, gaining a seventy per-cent market share in some territories.

By that time Sony had embarked on its expansion programme through the acquisition of US software companies. Of these, the most important and lucrative were CBS Records, Columbia Pictures and later, ATV Music. Once the cell-phone revolution was in full swing, a new enterprise, Sony Ericsson, was formed, a merger between European cutting-edge, mobile-phone hardware and Japanese know-how. Such has been the success of Sony Ericsson that at the end of 2005, its share-price performance led to a rise in the total value of the Tokyo stock exchange. With these purchases providing revenue-generating products, Sony would never be caught short in the software department again. Except that the accountants now had to deal with artists, who are unpredictable, a characteristic which annoyed some of the more conservative Sony executives. But worse, far worse, was just over the horizon.

At the Consumer Electronics Show (CES) in Las Vegas in January 2006, two huge corporations went head-to-head. The battle was over new, competing systems of video delivery. The prize; to own the world-wide format for High Definition Television and High Capacity Video Discs, which will define the next generation of TV viewing. Sony originally thought it had the market to itself with its new Blu-Ray system. In order to avoid the debacle of the video wars of the seventies, Sony made sure it had access not only to its own catalogue of software, which after fifteen years of acquisitions was gargantuan, but also to those of a number of other Hollywood studios.

There was, however, a new kid on the block who wasn't around in the 1970s. He goes by the name of Bill Gates. At the CES, Gates' hugely successful corporation, Microsoft, weighed-in with its own system, HD-DVD. Unfortunately for consumers, the two formats are incompatible. Microsoft was already making inroads into Sony's Playstation market-share with its X-Box and now the company unveiled a plan to put HD-DVD into its console. Toshiba announced production of an HD-DVD player which would hit US shops by March 2006. The first two models were to retail at $499 and $799. In contrast, so keen were those at Sony to tie up Hollywood studios, they did not pay enough attention either to price or the timing of the availability of their product. The first Blu-Ray machine, a Pioneer Elite, would not be ready until summer 2006 at the earliest and would cost $1800, with a cheaper Samsung model following later at around $1000. Microsoft also had support from such companies such as Intel and Hewlett-Packard. Sony still held many cards, it garnered the backing of Dell and Apple, for instance, but instead of a clear route to the future, Sony now faced a fight. High definition is the coming trend and high capacity video can hold much more information than conventional systems. The rewards for the winners of this war are immense, for the losers, who knows?

Ted Schadler, an analyst at Forrester Research, a Boston-based institution, carried out a re-evaluation of the prospects for Sony's system after the CES. He still thought Blu-Ray would win out in the end. Microsoft's entrance into the market, he said, would 'prolong the battle'. But he also declared that because the two systems were incompatible, 'Eventually, they both lose'. Perhaps Bill Gates already recognised this. Looking ahead, beyond high definition technology, he said: 'This is the last physical format there will ever be. Everything is going to be streamed directly or on a hard disk.'

Unfortunately for Sony, its profits had fallen by 25% in the preceding four or five years to 2005. It had once again been hit by a whirlwind of ill-fortune, most being problems of its own making. For years, Sony had been making money hand over fist with its Walkman and Playstation products. Complacency set in. Either that or the company's attention was diverted by its move into software. Whatever the case, Sony was not ready for the product that would make the Walkman (later the Discman) obsolete virtually overnight, Apple's amazing ipod. Suddenly, at a time of near-recession in the far-east, two of Sony's major revenue-streams were under threat by a brace of US corporations, Microsoft and Apple, whose new creations hit Sony hard. In the downturn, thousands of Sony employees world-wide would be made redundant. So much for the new Japanese model, where workers were supposed to have a job for life. And so much for the Americans 'losing their edge'.

Yet an even more revolutionary event had taken place as the true extent of Sony's losses became clear. In the late 1990s, Norio Ohga had passed the reigns to Nobuyuki Idei, who, although he emerged from Sony's marketing division, was steeped in the corporation's traditional business, the design and manufacture of consumer electronics. Ohga's role became ceremonial, apart from overseeing the Jackson business, and he retired as Chairman of the Board in 2003, just as *Living with Michael Jackson* was broadcast. Ohga and Morita had seen Sony reach the heights. In the latter days of Ohga's rule and later, under the auspices of Idei, Sony was no longer the force it had once been and was in no position to turn itself around. In response, the board took the momentous decision to give the top job to a non-Japanese for the first time. Sir Howard Stringer, a Welsh-American who had run the US Entertainment division, assumed the mantle of leader.

What kept Sony going during this period were the profits posted by the companies bought under Ohga's vision, the American and later world-wide software companies like CBS Records and Columbia Pictures. Even there, though, no one had really replaced the profit-machine that constituted Walter Yetnikoff's years in command. Tommy Mottola tried but Sony seemed behind the curve and over-reliant on the repackaging of its back catalogue. It now fell to an American to bring the harsh reality of neo-liberal economics to the most venerable of all Japanese multi-nationals.

On the face of it, as Sir Howard got to work, Sony's outlook was not too bad. This view was enhanced when the corporation announced its fourth quarter figures for 2005. The results were talked up because they were better than expected. Net profit had gone up 17% to $1.4 billion for the quarter, while sales jumped 10%. Things were not as rosy as they appeared, however. Microsoft's profits for the same period were $2 billion and rising. Moreover, Sony's figures could not be seen as part of an upward trend. Costs were being cut through trimming the workforce but no one really knew which way things would go once the reduction in employee numbers worked its way through the system.

Sony's woes could not simply be put down to the troubled performance of the Japanese economy. While Sony was experiencing its problems, another Japanese giant, Toyota, was becoming the number one automobile manufacturer in the world. As analyst, David Robertson reported in summer 2006: 'Its (Toyota's) market capitalisation of $188 billion dwarfs the $17.9 billion value of General Motors – and indeed exceeds the combined market values of GM, Ford, Volkswagen, Citroen-Peugeot and Daimler-Chrysler.' In August 2006, Toyota's second quarter profits reached 3.4 billion. And it wasn't just Toyota that was performing well. Honda announced a massive investment in the production of a new seven-seat aeroplane, which it calls the micro-jet.

Much of Sony's hopes for the future were pinned on the Playstation 3, but before the new console could hit the shops, Microsoft produced its X-Box 360. The 360 sold out within hours of its release to retail outlets. In Northern Europe, X-Box's chief, Neil Thompson, spoke of shortages. 'I don't anticipate people being able to just walk into a retailer to pick one up,' he said confidently in December 2005, just as the 360 was released in Europe. The PS3 was scheduled to be released in Japan in spring 2006 but as the new year got under way, there was mounting speculation in the press concerning possible technical problems in the PS3's specifications. In February, a Sony spokesperson told the Reuters news agency that 'We're aiming for spring but we haven't announced specific regions (where the PS3 was to go on sale).' Part of the problem was the need, now that Microsoft had stolen a march by incorporating HD-DVD in its consoles, to try to give the PS3 a Blu-Ray DVD drive. 'We're waiting for them (the drive specs) until the last possible minute,' the spokesperson continued, 'but the launch could be pushed back if they're not decided soon.' Sony seemed wrong-footed by Microsoft and the barnstorming PR which normally accompanied Sony's products was faltering.

The 360 raised the bar in terms of console technology. Sony promised that the PS3 would deliver 'crystal-clear graphics, a high-speed internet connection with audio and video streaming, digital photo storage and a state-of-the-art (Blu-Ray) DVD drive.' In short, it was to be the first home entertainment box to include all functions previously carried out by separate pieces of equipment – consoles and DVD players. To accomplish all this needed lots of new technology. For example, a new chip, much more powerful than the Pentium 4 processor, was due to be installed. All this not only delayed the launch of the PS3, it also had implications for the price of the console and therefore Sony's profits. In the USA, the X-Box sold for $400 on launch. The expected new Nintendo console, the Revolution (the name was later, incomprehensibly, changed to Wii), is priced around $300. In a document produced by the financial giant, Merill Lynch, it was stated that the inclusion of so much new technology made the PS3 'prohibitively expensive to make.' The cost of each PS3, according to Merill Lynch, was likely to be $900 on launch. To be competitive on price, Sony would have to take a huge loss on each console sold. If it kept the price up to realistic levels, the company would be sure to lose significant market share to its rivals. Sony shares lost 3% of their value on the Tokyo stock exchange when these problems became public knowledge.

In March, the fears over the PS3 were finally realised when Sony announced that its promised spring launch was to be postponed for at least six months. The head of Sony's video games division, Ken Kutaragi, was remorseful. 'I would like to apologise for the delay,' he said. 'I have been cautious because many people are banking on the potential of next-generation DVD.' What Kutaragi was saying was that the success of both the PS3 and the Blu-Ray DVD system were inextricably linked. The trouble was that Sony faced competition from Microsoft on both fronts. And if, as Kutaragi says, many people are 'banking' on the potential of next-generation DVD, where does that leave Sony? It is not certain whether Sony's format will win the day. The statement hardly filled the market with confidence.

By May 2006, the 360 had sold more than three million units. Sony could not allow the situation to drift any further. At the Electronic Entertainment expo in Los Angeles that month the company decided to fight back by giving a demonstration of the PS3 and announcing when it would be available in the shops. The event did not go well. The PS3 would not be ready until November, the price would be a full $100 more than the 360, while the price of an additional controller (necessary for any self-respecting gamer) had not been decided. By the time the PS3 is available, Microsoft could well have shifted twelve million of the 360. Sony's Vice President of computer entertainment, Phil Harrison, tried to put a brave face on things, saying 'We are really trying to push what this machine is capable of.' Paul Jackson, a videogame analyst at Forrester Research, was also upbeat, but there was a caveat in what he had to say. 'There's a good chance that if they can get it right, it will be the biggest game console launch ever.' If they can get it right. That will require the sure touch that seems to have deserted Sony in recent years.

One of Sir Howard Stringer's first decisions when he took over was to axe a Sony icon, Aibo the robot dog. Aibo, created by Sony's robotics division, which was also shut down by Stringer, was used in Sony's publicity, in its promotional literature and it was featured heavily on the company's website. It did not produce much in the way of profits though, despite having sold 150,000, mainly in Japan. A third generation Aibo was in the pipeline but Stringer was not impressed. In the new austere circumstances, the man at the top wanted the corporation to concentrate on more profitable ventures. Stringer showed his ruthless side when he took the decision to kill off Aibo and its creators. But in the process he severed an important link to the past, to the time when Sony's fortunes were built on cutting-edge research. Stringer also cut back on the plasma television operation. Developing plasma technology had swallowed huge amounts of cash and the resulting product, while technically brilliant, has proved expensive and was overtaken by flat-screen LCD televisions, which serve much the same function but are cheaper. Instead, Stringer decided to pin Sony's hopes on a new television, the Bravia, seen within the corporation as the true successor to the innovative Trinitron. The signs are that Sony could have a winner with the Bravia but it will take years before that is known for sure.

As well as this downsizing, Stringer had to deal with an investigation into Sony's business practices by the British Office of Fair Trading in 2005. Before long, the European Union also became involved. The investigation was set up to look into allegations that Sony was operating a duel-price scheme, charging a differential between high-street retailers and online suppliers. Sony's spokesman in the UK, Bill Vestey, said the company was merely helping shops which 'invested in the brand'. An EU Commission spokesperson was more forthright, declaring, 'This scheme is illegal, or should be.' At the time of writing, there has been no outcome to the case. The European Union competition authorities also decided to take a look at the merger between Sony's record division and the German media group Bertelsmann. Again, those investigations are ongoing.

In this environment it was more important than ever that the entertainment division increased its profits. Ohga's prescience had saved the company from a terrible fate when he launched into records, films and computer games. These operations have provided significant earnings in recent years, while Sony's core products have faced stiff competition.

As Sony blazed the trail, the global record business began to be concentrated in fewer and fewer hands. And they are the dead hands of accountants. The days of outrage, personified by Walter Yetnikoff, were soon a distant memory. From the 1950s to the 1990s, large numbers of independent record labels existed alongside the major companies. Indeed, the independents negotiated deals with the majors for their record-pressing operations and the distribution of their records to shops. Throughout that period both majors and independents benefited from the arrangement. The independents tended to be closer to the grass roots and would often be at the forefront of new music, while the majors could afford the sums necessary to sustain or internationalise an artist's career. There were also a number of middle-sized labels, often run by managers or entrepreneurs. Robert Stigwood set up one of these, RSO Records, as did Chris Blackwell (who brought Bob Marley to a world-wide audience) with Island Records. Angie Guest and I owned an independent record label ourselves in the late 1970s and early 1980s.

Over the last ten years, however, with the rise of globalism and the thirst for takeovers and mergers, most of the independents have either gone to the wall or been swallowed up by the majors. Stax, Monument, Chrysalis, Charisma, Immediate, the list of lost labels is endless. Gradually, most independents were forced out of the marketplace. Not content with that, the majors then started to eat each other. Sony merged its record business with that of Bertelsmann, forming Sony BMG. The new company is the second biggest record company in the world behind Universal. Third, globally, is EMI, the last of the old British majors. EMI has been assiduously seeking for some years to takeover the company in fourth place, Warner Brothers. If EMI succeeds, there will be only three major record companies left. Warners has earnestly resisted EMI's overtures but at one point in 2006 the US company tried to turn the tables by making a bid to purchase EMI. It was a pathetic exercise, however. At present, the outcome of the courtship is unknown. In order to stave off the possible takeover, Warners were thrashing about trying to do anything they could to preserve their independence. They even overthrew a long-standing policy and decided to get into the Russian market, which is beset with problems of piracy.

In the meantime, online downloading offers the possibility of the wheel turning full circle. Small operations can once again make their music available to the masses themselves. However, the majors, who at first failed to see the impact of downloading, tried to stop it when they couldn't avoid it any more. They even formed a ludicrous pseudo-police force to take kids to court for free file-sharing. These same people probably spent their youth taping vinyl records onto cassettes. Now, they are starting to monopolise the downloading industry too. There seems to be no stopping the roll of these juggernauts.

Sony, desperate to preserve its global position in a number of areas, could not afford any damage to its revenue-producing activities in the music business. It would soon be time to grab full control of what is probably the single most lucrative song catalogue in the world, Sony ATV.

9

HOW DO YOU TELL?

In a dramatic piece of theatre, Tom Sneddon managed to produce one last twist to the proceedings in Santa Maria. After the defence had finished presenting its case, he made yet another application to the court. He received permission from Judge Melville to play a videotape showing Gavin Arvizo telling prosecutors that Michael Jackson molested him. The tape was recorded when Gavin first changed his story from his earlier outright denials of any inappropriate behaviour by Jackson. Now he became the star's chief accuser. Once Gavin Arvizo was out of Jackson's influence he became subject to legal advice. In such a situation any lawyer worth his fee would ask himself 'who can I sue?' Gavin Arvizo could sue Michael Jackson for a large amount of money. That would be easier if Jackson was convicted in a criminal case first. As Gavin passed into the hands of the prosecutors of Santa Barbara, his account of what happened shifted from a statement which supported Michael Jackson's interests to one that served Tom Sneddon's. The youngster did not reveal anything on-screen he hadn't already said on the witness stand but Sneddon hoped that by ending the trial with the recording, it would focus the attention of the jurors on Gavin's plight and his explicit descriptions of his sexual molestation. It might also mitigate the disastrous appearance of Sneddon's final witness, Debbie Rowe.

Once again pundits and legal experts overreacted, calling the tape a devastating blow. A former San Francisco prosecutor, Jim Hammer, told television viewers: 'He (Jackson) is in the greatest peril that he has been in throughout the entire trial. It was his lawyers' worst nightmare for the trial to end like this, with that boy's voice ringing in the jury's ears.' There seemed to be ex-prosecutors sprouting everywhere. Another one, called Craig Smith, who should have known better since he used to ply his trade in Santa Barbara County, thought Mesereau had made a big mistake in showing a video in which Jackson compared himself to Mother Theresa.

'This is Santa Maria,' he said, displaying the depth of his local knowledge. 'This is a small town. This is not a place all that accepting of diversity or of people who have different lifestyles.'

The jury finally retired to consider its verdict on June 2, 2005. Within a day, the television network for which Martin Bashir works, ABC, aired a tape of an interview with Michael Jackson, made five years earlier. In it, Jackson said: 'If I was told I could never see another child I would kill myself. I swear to you because I have nothing else to live for.' This tape was made by a so-called friend and 'spiritual advisor' to Jackson, Rabbi Shmuley Boteach. The rabbi followed up with a number of television interviews of his own. Perhaps Boteach realised his services would be more newsworthy if he sexed up his story a little, because on more than one occasion during his television interviews he came close to saying he thought Jackson was guilty. As news from the trial itself dried up once the jury was out, all manner of strange characters and stories were wheeled out to fill the vacuum.

The prosecution appeared confident in public. So much so, they once again got the tone completely wrong. Six days into the jury's deliberations, a party was thrown at the most expensive restaurant in town. Attending were Tom Sneddon, Ron Zonen, Gordon Auchincloss, plus their wives, family and friends. They were observed by fellow diners celebrating, as if they had already won the case. One customer said: 'They were toasting their success against Michael Jackson. Even though the jury is still out, everyone was in party mood and Sneddon spent the night with a broad smile across his face.'

It was a *faux pas* of major proportions. The Jackson camp was furious when the news leaked out. The singer had decamped to Neverland to await the verdict and from there Jackson's spokesperson was livid and expressed the singer's bitterness. 'For Sneddon and his team to party in public while Michael sweats it out is a disgrace,' the spokesperson railed. 'While they were out popping champagne corks, he was shaking and trembling and his family had to beg him to eat. Michael is in a terrible state. He is at the lowest ebb of his life and has barely slept. His back is in agony and he's been taking pain killers to help.' Once again, media pundits were hopelessly wide of the mark in their interpretations. While remaining careful to not condone the way Sneddon conducted his celebrations, they saw it as confirmation of their collective opinion that the jury would do the right thing and find Jackson guilty. After all, the prosecutors must know something.

The jury, as we know, saw things differently. After two weeks considering the evidence, they returned their now famous verdicts. As is customary in high-profile trials in the USA, the jurors gave a press conference once their verdict was in. It was the first chance any of us had to glean how their thought processes had worked. Up to then, everything was based on interpretation of the body language displayed by members of the jury. Various opinions were delivered by psychologists who specialise in this esoteric outpost of the discipline. Their numbers seemed to be growing in correlation to the increased desperation of the media to fill in the gaps. Believe it or not, there is still a good living to be made by what is, essentially, no different to crystal ball-gazing, although these days it is dressed up as science.

Many jurors said they were influenced by the negative attitude of Janet Arvizo. 'I disliked it intensely when she snapped her fingers at us,' one juror said. This was a reference to one of Arvizo's many outpourings, directed at Jackson, the judge, the jury or anyone else for that matter. Another juror said: 'She never took her eyes off us. I was uncomfortable with that.' It seemed the lawyers I spoke to about the trial were closer to jury's feelings than any number of media experts. When asked if they accepted Tom Mesereau's argument that the accusers were 'thieves and scam artists,' a jury member replied: 'The thought was definitely there. Things just didn't add up.'

Tom Sneddon looked stunned when the verdicts were read out. He had spent so much time on the details of the charges, this outcome must have seemed impossible. When Judge Melville, in his instructions to the jury, allowed a lesser charge on the alcohol counts, so that it wasn't necessary to find that Jackson administered the drinks to further his attempts at abuse, Sneddon thought he had the singer where he wanted him. Now the jury had said they didn't believe Jackson had given alcohol to the Arvizo children at all. Their conclusions were the same as those of Paul Russell when he spoke to me at Wentworth. Russell was someone who knew Jackson and he had queried the alcohol charges, now a jury, none of whose members was acquainted with the King of Pop, had come to the same conclusion. Tom Sneddon failed to see any of that. He has never given a credible explanation for his degree of certitude.

Chapter 9

In the immediate aftermath of the trial, Sneddon did his best to play the role of unruffled elder statesman. Few were taken in. At his post-trial press conference, he was forced on to the defensive and had to justify his motives. At first he blamed the celebrity factor. Presumably, Sneddon believed that if the defendant had been an ordinary member of the public, who could not afford the brilliant and expensive attorneys attending to Jackson, the prosecutors could have railroaded him. This was a grave slur on the members of the jury, portraying them as people incapable of concentrating on the evidence, so mesmerised were they by their close proximity to a star. Apart from that explanation, Sneddon stuck to the same line he had taken from the beginning, saying, 'Obviously, we're disappointed. But my past history with Michael Jackson had absolutely, unequivocally nothing to do with this case.' Sneddon then turned defiant, stating: 'I'm not going to look back and apologise for anything we have done. We did what we did for the right reasons. We thought we had a good case this time.'

Whatever he said, the Mad Dog had all but destroyed Michael Jackson's career. If that was his aim, he succeeded totally. As Max Clifford put it, 'I'm not surprised at the verdict but I think a lot of things came out in the trial which have left a bad taste in the mouth of the general public.' That didn't satisfy Sneddon, however. He wanted Jackson to do jail time and he will go to his grave with that obsession unrequited.

Jackson's high-profile supporters were quick to blame the media for the prejudice of much of the reporting. Revd Al Sharpton, who had been present when Jackson aimed his 'very, very devilish' insult at Tommy Mottola, was first into the fray. 'Michael Jackson's reputation has been damaged severely,' he began, 'but the criminal justice system has worked this time... The jury said the evidence wasn't there and they acquitted him. They showed tremendous courage.' The media, by contrast had, according to the reverend, 'lynched' the singer. Revd Jesse Jackson believed the star had suffered two trials, one in the courtroom the other in the media. 'Michael Jackson,' he said, 'has been convicted in many newsrooms.'

Elizabeth Taylor, who Tom Mesereau said would be a defence witness but who in the end did not take the stand, had been distancing herself from the singer since the Martin Bashir documentary. As one of Jackson's greatest friends and supporters, her absence was the subject of much comment. Now the movie star was fulsome in her praise of her friend and disparaging in her loathing for those who had persecuted him. 'I know he's innocent and I hope they all eat crow,' she said. Debbie Rowe, whose testimony had done much to undermine Sneddon's case, made her own contribution. 'I would never have married a paedophile,' she explained.

None of this was enough for a still-rabid media. They latched on to anything the jurors said which could be spun in a way that cast doubt on the verdict. The British press are experts at this. The *London Evening Standard* ran a huge front page headline, which screamed: 'Jackson Jury Shock. They suspected he was a boy molester but did not have enough evidence to convict.' The *Standard* based its story on the words of two jurors. One, the foreman, Paul Rodriguez said: 'The allegations of past abuse were considered credible to some extent. There are not too many grown men we know that would sleep with children but we had to base it (the verdict) on the evidence presented to us. There were a lot of things lacking.' The other juror, Raymond Hultman, said much the same: 'I cannot believe that this man could sleep in the same bedroom for 365 straight days (a reference to the testimony of one of the nine 'third party' witnesses who gave evidence of Jackson's supposed 'similar pattern' behaviour) and not do something more than just watch television and eat popcorn, I mean, that doesn't make sense to me. But that doesn't make him guilty of the charges that were presented in this case and that's where we had to make our decision. That's not to say he's an innocent man. He's just not guilty of the crimes he's been charged with.'

These statements sound eminently sensible to me, not shocking at all. It shows the jury taking their obligations seriously. They might have harboured doubts, prejudices and feelings but they stuck to their appointed task and based their findings on the evidence in front of them. Surely, the jurors' comments said more about the prosecution's presentation than it did about the actual guilt or innocence of Michael Jackson.

The *Daily Express*, another British newspaper, went even further than the Evening Standard. Its headline said: 'Jurors: We think he abused children.' To my knowledge no juror actually said those words and they weren't put in quotes by the newspaper. It was pure spin. The newspaper repeated the words of the two jurors quoted in the *Evening Standard* but added the thoughts of another juror, Eleanor Cook, who said: 'We had our suspicions but we couldn't judge on that because it wasn't what we were there to do.' Cook's words again display the jury's conscientiousness, an attribute the headline writers would have done well to emulate.

The most important information in the *Express*'s story was tucked away in the middle of the piece. This is what it said. 'Jurors revealed that a poll taken among themselves early in their deliberations showed that all but three members believed the pop star was innocent. The doubters were eventually convinced by their colleagues to clear the singer of all ten charges.' That hardly fits with the lurid headline, indeed it contradicts it completely. It sounds as if Rodriguez, Hultman and Cook were the three original dissenters but judging by their words even they appeared happy with the eventual outcome.

All the other jurors who were prepared to speak were scathing in their condemnation of the prosecution's witnesses. A female juror who did not wish to be identified condemned Janet Arvizo, saying, 'I cannot understand the values Mrs Arvizo taught her children. I would not want any of my children to lie for their own gain.' Another, Pauline Coccoz, a mother of three, said: 'What mother in her right mind would freely volunteer your child to sleep with someone and not so much just Michael Jackson but anyone for that matter?'

The British press may have been the worst offenders, they generally are, but their approach was mirrored the world over. It was left to the unlikeliest of civil rights defenders, the US publication, *The National Enquirer*, to break the consensus, running a story based around statements made by Jackson family members to the effect that Michael Jackson had been framed and was the victim of a vendetta on the part of Tom Sneddon and the Santa Barbara DA's office.

In fact Sneddon, by overreaching himself, blew the case. If he had a jury as sympathetic to his argument as he believed and as the media were telling him, how could he have failed so miserably? Yet fail he did, spectacularly. Juror Hultman summed it up better than any journalist when he said: 'The prosecution presented evidence that Jackson had a pattern of inappropriate behaviour with boys but not with Gavin Arvizo.' In that case, why did Sneddon not charge Jackson with offences relating to the other boys? One reason was the lack of direct evidence, but it is also the case that the Arvizo allegations fitted his view that the abuse occurred during the conspiracy, which was entered into because of the dreadful publicity following the broadcast of *Living with Michael Jackson*. That, according to Sneddon, had occurred because of Jackson's financial woes. If there were charges brought concerning any other boys, the financial situation could not have been responsible and Sneddon, for reasons best known to himself, had hung his whole case on the star being close to 'bankruptcy'.

While the press went for spin rather than accurate reporting, some US lawyers who had always been suspicious about the prosecution's case, came forward to reassert their analyses. A well-known American defence attorney, Ted Cassman, had this to say: 'The defence allegations against the mother may have fitted a preconception among the jurors. Many people believe that celebrities are easy targets so there is almost a presumption that a celebrity is someone who could be targeted.' Michael Brennan, a professor of law at the University of Southern California, said: 'If your case is about an adult male molesting a male child, you put on that case. The conspiracy case was not necessary and what it did was force the prosecution to put on the mother, who in turn was a disaster.'

Just like Jordan Chandler ten years previously, Gavin Arvizo now had to live his life as best he could. Unlike Chandler, though, there would be no $20 million to cushion the blow, although he has until he is twenty years-old to bring a civil case against Michael Jackson. It is nevertheless horrendous to contemplate what his future may hold. One newspaper, for instance, called him a 'conniving liar'. How can a young teenager be expected to live with that hanging around his neck? Meanwhile, Gavin's mother faced charges of welfare fraud and possible action by a chain store to recover losses they sustained when she sued them.

Tom Sneddon took a big hit to his reputation and probably an even bigger hit to his pride. He found out that when he lost, there really was no upside. His conspiracy theory, based on the supposed imminent financial collapse of Jackson, verified by his forensic accountant, had exploded in his face. He could, however, slip into his well-provided-for retirement, safe in the knowledge of his moral superiority.

The response to Martin Bashir has been more equivocal. Having been first on the stand, he was largely forgotten by the time the verdict was returned. He certainly didn't suffer any penalty for his refusal to answer questions, nor does he appear to be any less regarded at ABC. But perhaps the peak of his career is now behind him. At the time of writing there is a sort-of dormant law suit outstanding against Bashir in London, where Jackson's lawyers have filed for damages arising out of *Living with Michael Jackson*.

Tom Mesereau, was, as ever, supportive and spoke for Michael Jackson during an appearance on NBC Television. Admitting that it had been a 'grave mistake' to share his bedroom with Gavin Arvizo, Mersereau went on to say, 'He's not going to do that anymore. He's not going to make himself vulnerable to this anymore. Michael Jackson has not molested anyone.' As for what the singer was going to do now, Mesereau said: 'He's going to take it one day at a time. It has been a terrible, terrible process for him.'

Jackson' trials, though, were by no means over. As Winston Churchill once said when the tide of the Second World War seemed to have turned in Britain's favour. 'This is not the end. It is not even the beginning of the end. Perhaps we can say it is the end of the beginning.'

Within days of the verdict, a California lawyer who had once represented Jordan Chandler, Gloria Allred, filed a request with the Santa Barbara Child Welfare Service to have Jackson's children, Prince Michael and Paris Michael, immediately removed from his custody. Allred appeared annoyed at the not guilty verdict and accused the welfare department of letting down Jackson's children by not removing them from his care while he was on trial. Somewhat opaquely, the lawyer justified her intervention by first impugning the jury, saying there had been enough evidence to convict the singer, then with the statement that 'Children of celebrities deserve the same protection as children of non-celebrities.' Whatever that meant, it did not auger well for Michael Jackson.

How do you tell who is a paedophile? Well, I don't know the answer to that any more than anyone else. I suppose in the Jackson case most would say it was obvious. Most, of course, except for the jury.

During the 1970s and 80s, I was the Managing Director of an independent record label called Different Records. We specialised in niche markets where the major companies were weak. In our case we bought the UK rights to some original reggae recordings from Jamaica, including seminal albums such as 'Forward on to Zion' by the Abyssinians and 'Revolutionary Dream', by Pablo Moses. Our records were pressed in the factory of one of the majors, Decca, while our distribution was divided between our own deals with various independent reggae retailers (many were one-man operations) who found it difficult to acquire accounts with major companies, and Selecta, the distribution arm of Decca, which supplied the main retail trade.

One day, Different's lawyer, a well-known music business attorney, Tony Seddon, introduced me and my then partner, Angie Guest, to Matt

Thompson-Royds, an old Etonian who dabbled in show business through his own company, Mystic Bird Productions. Thompson-Royds had been asked to find a record company which would be crazy enough to release a record by the choirboys of the most famous church in London, St Paul's Cathedral. A prestigious BBC Television arts strand called 'Arena' was producing a programme paying homage to the song 'My Way'. Although mostly associated with Frank Sinatra, the ballad was and is one of the most performed songs ever written. 'Arena' arranged for a number of different versions of the song to be recorded, some of which were at first glance unusual. The most outlandish was a performance by the choirboys of St Paul's. After all, 'My Way' is about someone approaching death while reflecting (vaingloriously) on their life. The Choirmaster, Barry Rose, asked Thompson-Royds to see if he could get the song released. Thompson-Royds, via Tony Seddon, came to me.

We recorded an album by the choirboys which went on to achieve some success. Before that, I noticed that one of the boy sopranos, Paul Phoenix, was blessed with perhaps the best natural voice I had ever heard. As a child, I sang myself, not in a church choir but in school choirs during my education and I worked with singers throughout my career in music. I knew what I was hearing. Meanwhile, Thompson-Royds came up with an idea of epic proportions. The BBC, in association with Paramount, was to make a seven-part television adaptation of *Tinker, Tailor, Soldier, Spy*, a cold war novel by the writer, John Le Carré. Its star was one of the greatest actors ever to come out of the United Kingdom, Sir Alec Guiness. Thompson-Royds had got wind of the fact that the incidental and theme music to the series was to be written by Geoffrey Burgon, one of those composers of modern classical music that everyone hates. The difference between Burgon and most of the rest, however, is that Burgon is a supremely talented composer who is especially good at creating just the right atmosphere with his compositions. For the theme to *Tinker, Tailor, Soldier, Spy*, Burgon came up with a haunting piece of music intended to be sung by a boy soprano, based on the Nunc Dimittis, a special psalm which is part if the daily Anglican service of Evening Prayer. Thompson-Royds wasted no time in convincing Barry Rose to let Different Records make and release the recording.

When *Tinker, Taylor, Soldier, Spy* hit the screens it was an immediate hit, both in Britain and around the world. Reviewers were as one in their praise of the theme tune and Geoffrey Burgon became as famous as it is possible to get for a composer of atonal music. At the Different Records office on Dover Street, in London's Mayfair, a momentum began to gather as demand for the record firmed up. Remember, this was a piece of obscure, modern classical music sung by a boy whose voice had not yet broken. I'm obviously not talking Little Jimmy Osmond here. Different was geared up to service a niche market, I wasn't totally certain we could handle mass demand. Then, one Friday afternoon, I received a call from Jonathan King.

Jonathan King was a fixture in the British music industry for over thirty years. His first and biggest-selling record as an artist was 'Everyone's Gone to the Moon', a massive world-wide hit in the mid-sixties. King had just graduated from Cambridge University and after his first hit or two became a record producer. His most famous tune in this capacity was the smash hit 'I'm Not in Love', by 10cc, in the mid-seventies. He hosted television programmes for years and was a radio DJ on the BBC's national pop music network, Radio One. He wrote columns for the press and organised one of Britain's entries in the Eurovision Song Contest. To say King was ubiquitous would be an understatement of gigantic proportions.

King was always possessed of an abundance of self-confidence. As time went on, however, it spilled over into arrogance and eventually, boorishness. He gave the impression of someone who came to believe his highly opinionated public statements were tantamount to fact simply because he uttered them. When I was told by my secretary that King was on the line I was fascinated by what he might have to say.

'Lynton, how are you?'

King was nothing if not effusive when he wanted something.

'Fine, Jonathan, fine. Long time no see. What can I do for you?

'I've been brought in by Sir Edward Lewis to revitalise Decca's A&R (Artists and Repertoire) department and restore the name of the company to prominence.'

'That's quite a task, Jonathan. No, it's more like one of the labours of Hercules,' I said (King always responded to a classical reference, particularly if it identified him with an ancient Greek hero).

Actually, I was not far wrong with my mention of Hercules. The Decca label, traditionally one of the greatest of British majors, was in a mess. Moreover, other parts of the Decca empire which in days gone by contributed significantly to its success, such as the manufacture of televisions, radios and tape recorders, had been eclipsed by the Japanese invasion. Even the company's renowned radar system was not making money and would soon be sold off to Racal Electronics. Worse, Decca's factories were beset by over-manning and low production. Its management, including the eighty year-old Chairman, Sir Edward Lewis, who had been one of the pioneers of the British record and electronics industry, was sadly out of touch. The record label was kept in business by the wonderful Decca classical music catalogue and the Moody Blues, whose success paid for the refurbishment of one of Decca's recording studios in London's West Hampstead district.

The Moody Blues notwithstanding, Decca's music division was moribund and had hardly produced a hit in years. In truth, the label which had given the world the Rolling Stones as well as the Moody Blues and many others, was, by the late 1970s, regarded as something of a joke. That was why independents like us negotiated good deals for ourselves with Decca's record-pressing factory (which was known for the quality of its pressings) and distribution operation. If they had to rely solely on Decca product, they would have had to lay off a significant number of workers. It was into this morbid environment that Jonathan King had now been thrust. Never one to underestimate his own abilities, King believed he could actually turn the company around from the drab office provided for him by Decca overlooking the south bank of the River Thames in central London.

'I want the Paul Phoenix record for Decca,' King continued.

'What?' I couldn't believe what I was hearing.

' "Nunc Dimittis" ', it's absolutely brilliant. It could be a big hit but only if it's on the Decca label.'

'What possible reason would I have for doing that?'

'Look, I'm going to play it as the first record on my radio show tomorrow. It's the best slot of the week, three minutes after midday.'

King was referring to a weekly BBC Radio One show he hosted each Saturday from midday to 2 p.m. In Britain in those days, Saturday lunchtime and afternoon fell in prime time. King's show drew a huge listenership.

'That's great, Jonathan, I'll make sure I'm tuned in.'

'You don't understand, Lynton, it must be on Decca.'

'But it's already on Different.'

'Name your price.'

It's not often you get to hear a statement like that. Name your price! But something in King's unctuous and overbearing manner was annoying me.

'It's not for sale Jonathan,' I responded.

'Don't be silly, name your price.'

'It's not for sale, what can I tell you.'

At that moment King began making thinly-veiled threats. 'Look,' he said, 'Your pressing and distribution are with Decca aren't they?'

'You know they are Jonathan, what's your point?'

'Well,' King replied, 'If you don't licence the record to Decca I could make sure you went down to the bottom of the list of priorities at the pressing plant and the distribution depot.'

Now I was really annoyed. But I wasn't impressed. At Different, we had developed our own relationships with Decca's factory and Selecta's warehouse. We knew the sales force and spoke to them often. If anyone was likely to be discriminated against, it was Decca, who were not providing either facility with enough work and hadn't been for years. The factory and warehouse managers were unlikely to succumb to the overtures of a 'here today, gone tomorrow' Jonathan King. King either had an inflated view of his own influence and power or he was bluffing. But Jonathan King was no fool. He must have wanted it pretty bad to chance his arm to that extent.

'Jonathan look, why don't you find your own hits,' I said, 'This record is not for sale,' King seemed to be getting the message but he was not best pleased. He started getting a bit manic. It was more than seemed reasonable even in the hot-house atmosphere of the record business. I got him off the phone as quick as I could. To be fair, the *contretemps* didn't stop King playing the record on his radio show. The records with the St Paul's Cathedral Choir went on to sell very nicely. We eventually licensed them to Charisma Records, who were responsible for Genesis, along with the off-shoots of that group, Peter Gabriel, Phil Collins and Mike & The Mechanics. Charisma organised a television advertising campaign and the album did remarkably good business. It was the first time a boy soprano had sold so many since the 1920s, when 'O for the Wings of a Dove' by Ernest Lough was a bestseller. It certainly paved the way for another boy soprano to become a star in the UK. Aled Jones, who shot to fame after winning a television talent contest, benefited greatly, in my opinion, from the trailblazing work of Paul Phoenix. 'Nunc Dimittis' went on to win an Ivor Novello award for the best TV theme of the year.

Jonathan King completely failed to revive Decca's fortunes and was soon on his way. Many years later I realised just why he was so keen to get his hands on Paul Phoenix. I should have known that his fondness for Ancient Greek mythology (and its attendant bisexuality) said more about King than it appeared to at first sight. King was arrested, convicted and imprisoned for having sexual relations with under-age boys going back decades. Everyone in the music business knew Jonathan King was gay, indeed he never made any secret of the fact. But a paedophile? I would never have known.

Michael Jackson's relationships with young boys were mulled over incessantly, both at his trial and in the media. One story that appeared nowhere, neither in the legal proceedings nor the accompanying comments, shows perhaps how atypical Jackson's behaviour actually is. In 1991, Jackson's Heal The World Foundation, which he established to help disadvantaged children around the world, was due to make a video of children in an orphanage in Romania. After the fall of the Eastern bloc and the execution of Romania's dictator, Nicolae Ceaucescu, those kids whose parents had abandoned them were left to their fate in terrible conditions in the orphanages.

As the idea for the video, which was to be used to seek help for the orphans, took shape, Jackson cast around for a director. One aspirant for the role was the respected British film maker, Gary Dyson. Dyson was summoned to Switzerland, where Jackson was performing live concerts, for an interview. The interview was to be conducted by Jackson, who would determine Dyson's suitability for the job. Unfortunately, as Dyson was on his way to the airport, Jackson was taken ill and had to cancel the Swiss gigs. For insurance purposes, two independent doctors were required to substantiate the extent of the singer's illness. A Swiss doctor came to examine the star and verified Jackson's malaise. The second doctor was based in Harley Street, London, so Jackson flew to Britain just as Dyson was boarding his plane to Geneva.

Although he was ill, Jackson still wanted the interview with Dyson to take place. He came up with a novel course of action. The members of Jackson's road crew were always encouraged to bring their children on tour and the star asked if a number of these children would interview Dyson in his stead. Dyson was somewhat taken aback but agreed. The children interviewed Dyson, liked him, and recommended him to Jackson. That's how Dyson got the job. Later, Dyson told me of his impression of Jackson when he eventually met him. 'I didn't speak to him for long,' Dyson said, 'but I was struck by his modesty, and the fact that he was not over the top.'

Maybe this story reveals nothing. Maybe it reveals a lot. How can you tell a paedophile? Perhaps I am naive but I don't know. What I do know is that when it comes to Michael Jackson, paedophile or not, a finding in his favour by the jury was of little help in reviving his flagging career. And the vultures weren't finished yet.

10

END GAME

While the jury was out in Santa Maria, I found myself once again in Paul Russell's house at Wentworth. As we looked out onto the verdant, tree-lined gardens Paul dropped another bombshell.

'You know he's no longer with Sony.'

Although Sony had been conspicuous by its absence from the Michael Jackson case, it had occurred to no one outside a handful of those in the know that the two had actually parted company or that the issue of Jackson's mechanical copyright had been resolved. In *The Magic and the Madness* J. Randy Taraborrelli leaves the matter with the statement that Michael Jackson 'managed to extricate' himself from Sony, who would release two further Jackson CDs. That is all the most authoritative book written about Michael Jackson has to say on the subject. No announcement was made, which would be the usual course of action in such a situation. Neither was the issue raised at Jackson's trial or in any of the media coverage. Strangely, Tom Sneddon, despite launching an all-out assault on Jackson over the issue of the singer's finances, never sought to bring Jackson's relationship with his record company into evidence. Even the forensic accountant had little to say on the matter. Yet in the music business, the really big stars' interaction with their record labels is of crucial importance and their finances are inextricably linked.

The way Paul Russell told it, there was a dispute between Jackson and his record company over how many songs were still 'owed' by Jackson to Sony under the 'billion dollar deal'. But Jackson was on trial and Sony was not minded to hold Jackson to its own interpretation of the contract, not least because it didn't want to be associated with the singer at all. What Sony wanted were the rights to 'Thriller' and the rest of Jackson's pantheon of hits. Sony used the disagreement over how many songs Jackson was contracted to deliver to get rid of him while retaining the mechanical copyright to his recordings. Sony magnanimously offered a compromise. Jackson could go, now. Other decisions made by the star around this time impeded his ability to utilise any leverage he might once have possessed. So many managers, lawyers, accountants and advisors were hired and fired by Jackson there was no one who could exercise the overall responsibility for the star's business interests. That nobody seemed to understand the necessity to initiate the Dunkirk process was an oversight too far and will cost Jackson dear down the years.

Jackson had no intention of making any more records for Sony. He thought he should fight over this principle. Although he didn't know it, he had no need to waste his energies since Sony didn't want any more of his material anyway. The company's insistence on holding Jackson to producing the 'missing' songs was a pretence designed to ensure that the singer fought the wrong battle. There was now only one option. Jackson was jettisoned as a Sony artist but the company, not the performer, would keep the mechanical copyright to all the old classics. The record company was happy to continue to pay Jackson his royalties. Sony was even prepared to raise the rate in certain circumstances. They also promised to revisit the issue of mechanical copyright at some unspecified date in the future. It was the best deal Jackson could get. In truth, he had to devote all his faculties to staying out of jail. With his concentration diverted, he thought the arrangement with Sony was a victory. There was to be no public statement. No one at Sony would crow. Neither would Jackson. For the moment, no one was saying anything, which must have been a unique period in the life of the King of Pop.

The last rites were read when Jackson's final Sony album, 'Number Ones', another compilation, dribbled out in 2003. The star's British fans, as ever, loyally propelled the album into the charts but, quite frankly, it bombed world-wide. All the issues that had exercised Jackson's mind in his dealings with Sony were now academic: Sony owned the copyrights, Jackson was out. It was that simple. Perhaps in a moment of reflection, Jackson might regret turning against the one person at Sony who was always on his side, had the power to look after his interests and was willing to use it. That person was Walter Yetnikoff. Michael Jackson, when he threw in his lot with Tommy Mottola and Norio Ohga, helping them when they wanted Yetnikoff out, paid for his betrayal by losing virtually every asset he possessed.

Paul Russell was not willing to be so forthright to reporters on the subject. In some ways that was my fault. As Kiki King and I drove to Wentworth with Les Molloy, I used the phrase, 'Sony has dropped Jackson.' When King put the same words to Russell he was unwilling to go that far, although it was the clear implication of what he was saying. Despite spending a lovely June day lazing on the lawn, while the *Mail on Sunday*'s photographer took pictures of Paul for an article, the newspaper decided they couldn't stand the story up. Well, that is what they told me. When Kiki King asked Sony if it were true that they had 'dropped Jacko', no one in any Sony office anywhere in the world would confirm or deny it. Normally when this occurs, British newspapers take it as confirmation of the story or at worst gives them the cover they need to run with it. This time, they departed from their own protocol. Why remains a mystery.

A few days later a report was carried in the *Guardian*, a British newspaper of some repute. After re-hashing the story of the loans from the Bank of America and the sale of Jackson's debt to Fortress, the two reporters who filed the story, Oliver Burkeman and David Teather, went on to state that Jackson had 'no new record contract.' For the first time this information was in the public domain. Strangely, the fact that the biggest-selling artist of his generation was now without a record deal failed to draw much by way of comment elsewhere.

Within a week the Jackson family, which had given conspicuous support to Michael throughout his trial, hired the Chumash Indian Casino in Santa Ynez, for a celebration party. Despite the presence of fans, family and even one of the jurors, Pauline Coccoz, the gathering was out of bounds to journalists. One who managed to breach the security cordon was escorted from the premises by the Chumash police force. Michael Jackson did not attend. Ensconced at Neverland, the singer had a number of problems with which he still had to deal.

The most pressing was the future of Neverland itself. Jackson was loath to sell the property but neither could he afford its upkeep. An eight month rearguard action ensued before, in March 2006, California State Labor Commission officers descended on the property and delivered an order banning any activity from taking place there. The commission acted because Neverland's employees were not being paid. There was an outstanding demand for $300,000 in unpaid wages plus fines, the total coming to nearly half a million dollars. It would not be long before all the animals were removed from the zoo. The amusement park's rides and sideshows were in the process of being dismantled or left to fall into a sad state of disrepair. It was an ignominious end to what had been the very public symbol of Jackson's superstardom. Its loss was equally emblematic. For a while the possibility existed that the Jackson family home itself would have to go as well but somehow, anyhow, Michael Jackson would not allow his mother, Katherine, to lose the home he had provided. However, the days of buying fantasy to replace reality were over.

In the immediate aftermath of the trial, Jackson was faced with perhaps the most important decision of his life. What was he going to do now? There was a new custody battle with Debbie Rowe over their children and enough lawsuits from various quarters to keep a small country's entire justice system occupied for years. The most urgent of these was a claim from a former business associate of Jackson's, Marc Shaffel, who insisted Jackson owed him millions of dollars in fees and un-repaid loans. Perhaps, Jackson must have mused, he should even contemplate leaving the shores of his own country for a while, till the heat died down. He could no longer work in his homeland and a period of silence was the only course left to him. But where would he go?

Enter Michael Jackson's saviour. Sheikh Abdullah bin Hamad al-Khalifa, son of the ruler of Bahrain, a tiny but wealthy desert kingdom in the Persian Gulf. Sheikh Abdullah, western educated and a long-time fan of Jackson's, offered the star the hospitality of his country, including a sumptuous home. In many ways it was the perfect solution for the singer. He could have gone to just about anywhere but in the Middle East he could at least put some distance between himself and the prying eyes of the world's press. In addition, by associating with a royal family, Jackson could keep up the aura of mega-success which has surrounded him for so much of his life.

From Bahrain, Jackson made numerous forays into the rest of the world, especially Europe. He was supposedly spotted in Frankfurt, Rome, Paris and London. He travelled with a much reduced retinue but still managed to keep a semblance of his publicity machine going. His main publicist, Raymone Bain, continues to make additions to Jackson's website and issue statements to the press from time to time. On September 12, three months after the end of the trial, it was announced that Jackson was to make a record for the victims of hurricane Katrina, which had recently devastated New Orleans.

A host of stars was lined up to appear with him, including Jay-Z, Mariah Carey, Missy Elliot (in my view the first musical genius of the 21st century), R. Kelly (who is currently facing sex charges of his own), Mary J. Blige and Snoop Dogg. A week later, Jackson telephoned the Associated Press to promote his involvement. As the months came and went there would be polite enquiries as to the progress of the song, a Jackson composition called 'From the Bottom of my Heart', but at the present time no record has been released and neither does it seem to be anywhere on the horizon.

In October, Jackson took his children to London, where they stayed at the Dorchester Hotel in Park Lane at the invitation of Sheikh Abdullah. They paid a very public visit to the theatre to see the stage version of the film, *Billy Elliot*. The two children's faces, were, as ever, covered. Jackson himself fell to the ground at one point in the meleé caused by fans and paparazzi. More fans besieged the star's hotel; it was almost like old times. However, although the purpose of the visit was ostensibly to record the song for Katrina victims, no word of any recording actually taking place slipped out onto the grapevine. Eventually, in April 2006, a story came out of Bahrain claiming Jackson had signed a new record deal and was ready to start recording a new album. On closer inspection, however, it wasn't quite the momentous occasion the press release conveyed. The record label Jackson signed to was one few have heard of, Two Seas Records. It transpired that the label is owned by Sheikh Abdullah. The singer issued a bland statement, saying, 'I am incredibly excited about my new venture and I am enjoying being back in the studio making music.' On a few rare occasions, such as the *Billy Elliot* show in London, it could appear like old times but it was, in truth, a long, long way from the heady days of yore.

In the meantime, behind the scenes, the vultures remained unsatisfied with their pickings. The mechanical copyright was merely the first course. Jackson's massive loan repayments and interest charges were set to ensure that pressure on the singer's assets was maximised.

The New York offices of Sony Music Entertainment no longer had any direct interest in Jackson and all those who had been around when he was at his peak were gone. Tommy Mottola hung around for a while after the 2002 Jackson insult shot him to prominence but his days were numbered and he left the corporation in 2003, not long after the broadcast of *Living with Michael Jackson*. By then, the only person with comprehensive knowledge of all that had occurred, Norio Ohga, had finally retired, removing Mottola's protection within the company. Once the leak of Jackson's financial circumstances to the Santa Barbara DA's office had taken place, Mottola was quickly shuffled off the stage.

Michael Jackson had again briefly threatened Sony's image, an extremely grave offence in the eyes of the Japanese corporation. Nevertheless, Jackson also represented an important opportunity to contribute significantly to any retrenchment plans. The installation of Sir Howard Stringer in the top job did not magic away Sony's problems. If anything, they were worse.

My sources within Sony told me that throughout the second half of 2005, after the Jackson trial, those in the know were happy simply to wait for the singer to default on his loans to Fortress. Their behind-the-scenes deals allowed them first refusal should Jackson be forced into selling any of his Sony ATV shares and they had been in talks with Fortress for some time about the issue. Where any duties of confidentiality or care now rested is impossible to say.

The financial situation at Sony was not improving. In the record division, for instance, there was trouble concerning the merger with the recording arm of the Bertelsmann Media Group (BMG), a German conglomerate of many years standing. The merger suited both parties at the time and created the world's second biggest record company. By the beginning of 2006, however, those running BMG were having second thoughts.

Twenty-five per cent of the whole Bertelsmann group is owned by a Belgian investment company, Groupe Bruxelles Lambert (GBL). GBL approached Bertelsmann to inform them that, as was its right in its agreement when it purchased the Bertelsmann shares, it wanted to list its stake on the Frankfurt Stock Exchange. Members of the reclusive Mohn family, who own most of Bertelsmann's stock, were horrified. When they sold their 25% stake to GBL, the family never believed that the Belgians would opt for the listing. The Mohns wished to keep Bertelsmann as a private company at all costs. Something had to be done.

Bertelsmann's CEO, Gunter Thielen, was tasked with finding out what parts of the company could be sold to raise money to buy back the 25% held by GBL. The most obvious candidate for disposal was Bertelsmann's stake in Sony BMG, which is worth some $2 billion as of mid-2006. Moreover, tensions had been building in the merged company for months at management level. The disputes contributed significantly to a sharp fall in turnover for Sony BMG in 2005. Its revenues were down more than 16%.

I had some experience myself with the problems within the new company. Ever since the days of CBS in the sixties, the manufacturing, distribution, accounts and royalties departments were located in the small town of Aylesbury, in Buckinghamshire, an hour north of the capital. I dealt with the same friendly and helpful personnel over many years. When Sony BMG was created, the factory and offices at Aylesbury were closed without warning. I only found out when I had occasion to contact the royalties department. The whole operation was moved to London, specifically to BMG's facility on Fulham High Street. A few of the old guard from Aylesbury survived but many, I found out, were gone. To my knowledge, no Sony artist was ever informed of these developments even after they had taken place. I found out by accident and I'm sure my case was no exception.

At a results briefing in Berlin, Bertelsmann revealed it had hired a US firm, Boston Consulting, to conduct a review of Bertelsmann's assets. Thielen all but ruled out any sale of its core businesses, saying he 'could not imagine' losing the book and magazine publishing empire which was Bertelsmann's original business, or RTL, Bertlesmann's most profitable division, which owns the European television network, Canal Plus, and the British television channel, Five. Given that the 25% owned by GBL is worth $6 billion, it is obvious that if the Mohn family desired to keep Bertelsmann private, its stake in Sony BMG would have to be sold.

Bertelsmann would have to offer its stake to Sony. Only if the Japanese turned it down could they sell it on the open market. But this was not what Sony had in mind when they merged their record company with BMG. They did not want a partner they had not chosen themselves but neither did they envisage paying out $2 billion not contemplated in their budgeting. Even giant multi-nationals have their limits.

Despite reducing turnover, the entertainment division was one of the few areas (along with Sony Ericsson, which contributed $250 million of profits in the last quarter of 2005) delivering consistent results. Games, films and music, the sectors into which Norio Ohga had guided the company, kept Sony buoyant. The American entertainment operation in particular outperformed every other Sony division, Although the music arm has never recovered totally from the downturn following the departure of Walter Yetnikoff, the games company (selling software and notwithstanding the problems with the PS3) peformed spectacularly. Nonetheless, one US subsidiary, Sony Pictures – the old Columbia Pictures – slipped to third place in the box office league table in 2005. The company failed to follow up its successes with *Charlie's Angels* and *Spiderman*, which had propelled Sony to the number one spot. Its hopes for 2006 were pinned on the success of *The Da Vinci Code* and the millionth picture in the James Bond franchise. Sony Pictures was not helped by the fact that it had two heads, Amy Pascal, responsible for commissioning movies, and Michael Lynton, overseeing the business side. Both report to Sir Howard Stringer.

In the event, though the *Da Vinci Code* made large profits, it was not the blockbuster the success of the book suggested it would be. Luckily for Sony Pictures, an unsung comedy movie, *Talladego: The Ballad of Ricky Bobby*, starring Will Ferrell, reached the top of the US box office in its first weekend of release in August, 2006. It managed to earn $47 million, more than three times the revenue of the second placed film, the animation movie, *Barnyard*. This, however, did not help move Sony out of the third place slot overall. The top two positions were still held by Disney's Buena Vista and Fox.

In the record business, more changes were occurring in the wider world which made it imperative for Sony to consolidate its position. EMI has been relentless in its pursuit of Warner Brothers. If the two do eventually get together, the new entity will be a real threat to Sony. In May, 2006, EMI made a new, improved offer for Warners of $4.2 billion. Although the approach was again rejected by the Warner Bros. board, few will bet against the eventual acquisition by EMI.

An aspiring music major, the Sanctuary group, which also went into artist management in what it called a '360 degrees business model', saw the value of its shares take a dive. In deep trouble since it acquired a record label, Urban, from the father of Beyoncé Knowles, the group got rid of its CEO and founder, Andy Taylor. Although the ex-Chairman of British Airways, Ted Ayling, was brought in to rescue the company, its ultimate failure would be sure to have a knock-on effect throughout the industry. Another Sony competitor, Disney, sold its ABC radio network for $2.7 billion dollars. Meanwhile, Viacom's MTV networks teamed up with the search engine company, Google, to distribute television clips of music videos through Google's internet advertising operation. These developments show just how quickly things change in the modern entertainment industry. It is now left to Sir Howard Stringer to try and keep Sony in the game.

One long-established major name in the sector, for instance, Philips, an old competitor of Sony's which briefly entered the video wars of the 1970s finally threw in the towel in 2006. Philips is fast becoming a 'lifestyle' brand, moving out of many of its traditional areas into such things as medical equipment. One of the newest machines now used in hospitals is the Philips Heart Start, a new defibrillator. These changes prompted Philips' Chief Executive, Gerard Kleisterlee, to say: 'In those areas of consumer electronics, it's winner takes all. The winner makes money for a while and all the others lose. That's not a very attractive proposition.'

During this period of upheaval, the four majors left standing were accused of payola in New York by the State Attorney General, Eliot Spitzer. Spitzer claimed to have gathered evidence proving that the companies abused their market positions by making secret payments to radio stations in return for airplay. A statement from Spitzer's office said the corporations also provided 'Financial benefits to obtain airplay and boost the chart position of (their) artists by bribing radio station employees with concert tickets, video games and hotel and airfare expenses.' In an amazing turn of events, none of the companies was prosecuted for their transgressions. Instead, Spitzer and the four corporations negotiated a series of fiscal penalties to keep the cases out of court. Sony's share of the fines came in at around $4 million.

If the four companies were indeed doing what the Attorney General accused them of – and in paying the fines they made certain admissions – then it is extremely unlikely they restricted their activities to one state. To date no equivalent investigation has been opened by the justice departments of other states.

Word reached Sony in late 2005 that Michael Jackson was making a last-ditch effort with Fortress to reschedule his debt and thus save the last of his big assets, Sony ATV. He had missed his monthly repayment in October and by December faced foreclosure. Fortress agreed to a meeting with Jackson's lawyers and his brother, Randy, to see if there was any way out. Jackson's team offered a 9.5% interest rate if the next payment could be postponed for six months. Fortress wanted 20%. As this was going on, one of Jackson's lawyers, Brent Ayscough, maintained everything was under control. 'There is no doomsday or anything like that,' he said, 'at the moment people are still talking.'

Sony's agreement had to be forthcoming when Michael Jackson took out his loans with the Bank of America. That was because they owned fifty per cent of Sony ATV. Any change of ownership of the debt, such as when it moved to Fortress, similarly had to be given Sony's OK. Now, Fortress would have to take soundings from Sony over any major rescheduling. They also informed Sony that Jackson had defaulted. In keeping with the old 'patient and determined' outlook of Akio Morita and Norio Ohga, Sony did not immediately spring into any great action. But the unofficial word from the corporation to Fortress was that Sony would not countenance any change in the repayment agreement. Fortress, caught between its wish to earn the extra interest, and the risk of a total default, which would tie up the courts for years, attempted to exert pressure on Sony.

The pressure wasn't really required. Sony was hard-balling but in the end its interests and those of Fortress coincided. In keeping with the old adage – my enemy's enemy is my friend – they both wanted Michael Jackson by the balls. This was the end game. The Japanese were in no hurry and they would get what they wanted. Negotiations between the parties meandered on into the New Year. Then, in April 2006, Sony struck. Once the position was reduced to its simplest options, Michael Jackson had no choice. To avoid foreclosure and therefore the loss of his entire stake in Sony ATV, Jackson agreed to sell half his shares to Sony, which would give the Japanese 75% of Sony ATV and control of the company. Fortress's risk was now underwritten by Sony. Moreover, the Japanese didn't even have to shell out any cash immediately. They could exercise their option at any time of their choosing up until 2009. That meant precious resources could be used to fight the High Definition war and sort out the Playstation 3 fiasco, while Sony ATV delivered increasing revenues. When conditions were right, it could take its extra 25%. It would not be surprising if Norio Ohga allowed himself a little chuckle at the news.

When the deal was made public, it was reported that 'Sony Executives' had been negotiating Jackson's loan refinancing with Citigroup bank, which forced Fortress to offer its own deal. In fact the 'executives' were Sony lawyers or members of Business Affairs. Sony's use of lawyers in these situations had served the company well down the years. Mickey Schulhof, the attorney Sony used to smooth its path in the USA and the first non-Japanese ever to be appointed to the main board of directors, was one such. But there had been many. Although he was not present at any of the meetings, the strategy had Norio Ohga's imprint all over it.

So, for the moment, Michael Jackson can, if he wishes, claim to have retained his stake in Sony ATV. But that would be more illusion. He is no longer on the board, has no say in the running of the company and has lost half of his stockholding. Finally, one of the biggest of golden eggs in the history of the music business, the publishing rights to Lennon and McCartney songs, had passed into the hands of the men from the land of the rising sun. For the Japanese, the future once again looked secure.

The future was by no means secure for Michael Jackson. As one of his advisors said, at the time of the refinancing talks, 'Frankly, he had no credibility with the financial markets.' It would be a long road back.

In May 2006, the showbiz reporter of the London *Daily Mirror*, Fiona Cummins, was photographed for the paper cuddling up to Michael Jackson. They met at the Harrods department store in London. Harrods' owner, Mohammad Al Fayed, who is a friend of Jackson's, provided his personal office for the meeting. Cummins reported that the singer 'seemed relaxed as he talked about rebuilding his tarnished career and his plans to create a new Neverland – in Britain'. Jackson himself said: 'I'm looking for a place to live. I've always liked the UK and I just love the fans here.' The air must have been thick with wishful thinking.

This story started out with a chance conversation in the house of a former Sony executive. At the time I was intrigued to see if I could shed any light on the paradox of Michael Jackson and the alcohol allegations that Paul Russell pointed out. I further wondered if it might help show Jackson's guilt or innocence of the charges he faced. I had no idea it would lead into the labyrinth that is the world of multi-national corporations, or through the murky waters of the entertainment business. Michael Jackson might well have brought most of his trials on himself. But trials he has had, there can be no argument about that. In the meantime, no one has brought the vultures to account for their nefarious roles in the saga.

In Stephen Hawking's book *A Brief History of Time*, the cosmologist writes about the possibility – or otherwise – of 'knowing the mind of God'. In my opinion it is as difficult to know the mind of another human being as it is any cosmic entity. We can estimate, interpret, rationalise or use our intuition. We might be right, we might be wrong. As far as Michael Jackson is concerned, I have not sought here to analyse his personality or find the elusive answers to the many questions that remain concerning his behaviour. When it comes to those we could do worse than follow the words of Paul Rodriguez, foreman of the jury in Santa Maria. However, when it comes to the rest of the cast – those who hide behind the respectability of corporations and who are all, no doubt, pillars of society – there can surely be only one verdict.

POSTSCRIPT

Michael Jackson

Entries continue to be made to Jackson's website, although they have begun to occur less often than in the immediate aftermath of his trial. His recording career seems to have stalled, despite the contract with Two Seas Records. As of August 2006, no Jackson CD is scheduled for release. Intriguingly, a reporter on the London *Daily Mirror* told me that a 'bidding war' was taking place for Jackson's contract. No evidence was offered for the assertion and I do not know if it is true. However, I have to say that I am extremely sceptical.

No matter what we think of Michael Jackson's behaviour or his character, I for one hope that he does record music again. Let's not forget he gave us some of the greatest pop music of all time. Can he do it again? Well, the odds must be against him but, then again, he has confounded us before. As Paul Russell said, "What he needs to do is go back to what made him so successful. He should forget the over-production and record something that shows off his voice, his unique singing style."

Michael Jackson is an outstanding musician, and I have immense respect for his talent. There is one track of his that to me will always remain outstandingly brilliant: 'Black Or White.'

Jackson still resides in Bahrain and still makes his regular forays into Europe. His financial problems, particularly in the USA, have not gone away. The custody battle with Debbie Rowe started to get nasty as 2006 progressed. We have heard little since the trial of Jackson's medical condition or his addiction to painkillers.

The Arvizo Family

Janet Arvizo is being investigated for welfare fraud. No decision on how the matter will progress has been forthcoming. As far as I know she is happily married and living in California. As for her unfortunate children, they have completely disappeared from the limelight. After what they have been through, perhaps that is for the best.

Postscript

The Sony Corporation

Sony still employs almost 150,000 people worldwide. It no longer bears even a passing resemblance to the company laid out in the Founding Prospectus. That corporation was supposed to keep its employee numbers to a minimum and distribute its profits among its workers. The Playstation 3 is conspicuous by its absence as of August 2006. The Blu-Ray High Definition system seems to be undergoing a rethink. Sony will, for the foreseeable future, be one of the three major record labels in the world. Its creative output, however, is a pale shadow of the force it was back in the days of CBS. Norio Ohga lives in quiet retirement in Japan.

Paul Russell

Paul Russell is retired, although you would never guess as much. The youthful-looking ex-executive involves himself in numerous projects in music and film. I hope one day to help him complete his autobiography.

Tommy Mottola

Tommy Mottola is semi-retired. He dabbles in music from time to time and was recently reported to be about to move to London. He has never spoken publicly of his role in the career of Michael Jackson and continues to maintain a dignified silence.

Walter Yetnikoff

Walter Yetnikoff remains an enigma.

Tom Sneddon

Tom Sneddon, Santa Barbara's longest-serving District Attorney, announced he would not be standing for re-election. He appears in the media from time to time and I would not be surprised if these one-off occasions turn into a new career of legal punditry. Do not rule out a book.

Tom Mesereau

Tom Mesereau, like any lawyer, has moved on to new cases, though none as public as the Jackson trial. It is alleged that he has been in dispute with the singer over unpaid legal bills.

Martin Bashir

Martin Bashir is still employed by ABC and held in great regard by the company. However, he has not, to date, come up with any more earth shattering 'current affairs films'.

Paul King

In a bizarre twist, in August 2006, Paul King, who appears briefly in chapter one, was reported to have been arrested and charged with assault after finding his long-time girlfriend in bed with the landlord of his local pub in Cornwall, England, where he has lived for some years

More Sony

Just to add to Sony's current maelstrom of woes, millions of lithium batteries made by the corporation for Apple and Dell computers had to be recalled in August 2006 because they were catching fire. Although the company tried to play down the situation, the eventual cost to Sony could well reach half-a-billion dollars.

LAST WORDS

In 1996, a six year-old beauty pageant queen, JonBenet Ramsey, was murdered in her home in Boulder, Colorado. From the beginning, the investigating authorities – the police and the Boulder DA – let it be known that they believed the hideous crime was carried out by one or other members of JonBenet's close family. Father, mother and even brother Burke, who was only nine at the time, came under what was termed the 'umbrella of suspicion'. For years, no one else was sought in connection with the killing.

It wasn't long before the media, in a feeding frenzy of epic proportions, decided that the case was open and shut. One or both parents did it. The only reason the Ramseys weren't charged, the story went, was because they were rich enough to hire good lawyers. They got away, literally, with murder. Documentaries (sorry, current affairs films), news reports and commentaries; all substantiated the case against the Ramseys.

Sound familiar?

Ten years later, in August 2006, John Karr, a 41 year-old US citizen and sometime teacher, was arrested in Thailand on suspicion of committing the murder after a new investigation by the Boulder DA, prompted by a journalist. At first, the media again thought the culprit was known but Karr became less convincing as a suspect when his confession was broadcast. At the time of writing, the FBI, having extradited him back to the USA was forced to let Karr go after DNA tests revealed he was unlikely to have committed the crime.

Whether or not Karr did it, now it has at last been recognised that someone other than a member of the Ramsey family could be guilty. I leave the last words to an old anti-war song, 'Where Have All The Flowers Gone'.

When will they ever learn...?

EPILOGUE

1.

As the whole world knows, Michael Jackson died on June 25 2009 at his rented home in Los Angeles. This is just about the only fact upon which most of us can agree. Once the story was out, the speculation machine swung into action with ever more lurid stories appearing in the world's press. At the same time something incredible happened. All round the world, people stopped what they were doing. Whatever the naysayers might claim in order to downplay the importance of Jackson's passing, the inhabitants of planet earth instinctively knew they had lost one of those artistic geniuses who come among us only too infrequently. Think Bach, Mozart, Beethoven, John Lennon and Marvin Gaye.

In writing this book I investigated how, in his later years, Michael Jackson was beset with trials and tribulations which, on the face of it, were unconnected to each other. There was the prosecution on child abuse charges, the downturn in record sales, the financial catastrophes and the struggles to retain ownership of assets such as Sony ATV, his back catalogue of recordings and Neverland. Yet far from being coincidental, everywhere we detected the hidden hand of the Sony Corporation attempting to orchestrate events. My account has never been refuted. If anything, the information I unearthed has gained ever more currency in the three years since the original book was published. Could it be that a continuation of the events I described, or something similar, was involved somehow in the singer's death? Given Michael Jackson's unbelievable life, that idea didn't seem so far-fetched as it otherwise might.

The televised memorial service from the Staples Center in Los Angeles was beamed round the world. In the UK, it was shown live on three channels. It was the same everywhere. In the wake of Jackson's death the airwaves, column inches and online postings were replete with tributes from hundreds of Jackson's colleagues, friends and family. There was the Rev. Al Sharpton, who organised the famous 'Go back to hell, Tommy' incident in New York, discussed in Chapter 4. There was the psychic, Uri

Geller, who had advised Jackson for a short period around the millennium, who took him to Exeter City Football club and who made the fateful introduction to Martin Bashir. There were employees past and present. There were all the family members. And there were many, many more.

Most of them turned up at the Staples Center. The absence of two of Jackson's closest friends – Elizabeth Taylor and Diana Ross – caused some comment but generally speaking there was a huge turnout. Except that there was one glaring omission. Where was any representative from the Sony Corporation? Where were the press conferences by present Sony executives bemoaning the death of their greatest artist. The memorial show was populated almost entirely with Motown stalwarts, Lionel Ritchie, Stevie Wonder, et al. Even Berry Gordy made a speech. Yet Michael Jackson spent a mere seven years with Motown, while he was signed to Sony for nigh on three decades. It was with Sony that he had his greatest triumphs. And wasn't there a degree of acrimony in the parting of the ways with Motown? Yet here was a virtual Motown-fest. It was the first in a chain of strange occurrences.

So the question is: why no Sony, who at first sight benefited most from Jackson's demise? In the days after the news rocked the world, sales of Michael Jackson's recordings went through the roof. In many territories his back catalogue comprised sixty percent of all music purchased. His videos were playing constantly on the music channels of the world. Sony was raking in money. My admittedly crude assessment is that within one month of his death, Michael Jackson's debt was all but eradicated, while Sony (and to a lesser extent Motown) cleared half a billion dollars. They were the great initial beneficiaries of Jackson's sudden departure from this earthly realm.

The honourable exception yet again was Paul Russell. From his retreat in Barbados he issued a eulogy to Jackson and spoke to the media to let them know how stunned and upset he was. He even provided some exclusive pictures of his years with the King of Pop which were printed in the British newspaper, the *Sunday People*. But that was it. Not a word emanated from the Japanese mega-corporation to suggest its executives were grieving with the rest of us. They must have been too busy rubbing their hands.

Sony had another reason to be cheerful. The original version of this book took great pains to unravel the story of Sony and Michael Jackson. One of the most important elements was the Sony ATV music publishing catalogue, which owns the rights to the songs of John Lennon and Paul

McCartney. However, the issue of ownership was not totally resolved by the time the book went to print, although some evidence had emerged. What happened was this.

Michael Jackson, after his acquittal, was forced to live a somewhat nomadic life. Shunned in his homeland, he wandered the world looking for some sort of salvation. The loans he had taken out would not go away, however, and the singer was forced to enter into an agreement with Sony, under which Sony assumed the debt in return for half of Jackson's shares in Sony ATV. The company also negotiated an option to purchase the remaining shares, an option which they could take up at any time of their choosing. These shares were transferred to a trust of which Jackson was a stakeholder. This convoluted structure enabled the King of Pop to say, with just-about honesty, that he still "owned" his half of Sony ATV. But in reality the whole company now belonged to Sony. Their desire to have complete control, put into motion years previously by Norio Ohga, was finally fulfilled.

The matter of ownership of Jackson's catalogue of recordings was put on the back-burner, and caused problems from time to time but Sony held all the aces. Then, with Michael Jackson finally out of the way permanently, Sony managed to be in a position to cash in on the man who first inspired its leaders to buy CBS in the first place and make all that money.

These days there is a macabre list of the yearly earnings of dead stars. Most years it is topped by Elvis Presley but other notables, such as John Lennon and Frank Sinatra make regular appearances. In 2008, Elvis earned some $55 million for his estate, $14 million of which was through merchandising his image and name. Michael Jackson will top Elvis's earnings easily and will head the 'dead stars' list by far for the next decade at least. Sony, no matter what problems might be experienced in other parts of its empire, will continue to benefit exponentially. Five years from now Sony's annual revenues from Michael Jackson related activities, including Sony ATV, will exceed five billion dollars.

Counter-intuitively, Michael Jackson's proposed comeback gigs in London could have put a dampener on Sony's profit stream. The singer's vast potential earnings from these concerts were set to transform his situation. When the gigs were announced, the world was stunned when almost three quarters of a million tickets were sold almost as soon as they became available. It was the biggest indication yet that Jackson could still occupy the top echelon of the showbiz pile. This was not what Sony wanted at all. They wanted a broken and weak Michael Jackson, one whom they could still control.

I shall return to this theme later. First I want to examine some of the claims and allegations that flourished in the immediate aftermath of Jackson's death. At first, it was assumed that Jackson suffered a fatal heart attack and that he died of natural causes. Meanwhile, the world's press chased anyone who had ever known the singer looking for stories, the more outrageous the better. Nowhere was this more so than in the British newspapers, most of which had a new Jackson headline every day. Some, such as *The Sun*, claimed to know the results of the autopsy, even before it was completed. The most authoritative provider of facts remained the American TMZ website, which was the first news outlet to report the star's death. TMZ repudiated *The Sun*'s take on the autopsy but gave some credence to a former Jackson nanny, Grace Rwaramba, who claimed that she had to "repeatedly pump his (Jackson's) stomach over the years" when he had too many prescription drugs in his system. Over the next couple of days most people focused on Jackson's legacy of great music. Others praised his skills as an innovative recording artist. The writer, Germaine Greer, told us that Jackson's contribution to dance was such that the way dance is now perceived and taught has changed to take account of his unique talents, technique and ability.

There were other elements arising from the death. Who would get custody of the children? Who would administer the estate? Where would he be buried? Uri Geller claimed he had begged the singer to give up prescription drugs, saying, "I tried to drum sense into his brain. I told him, 'Michael, you are going to kill yourself.'" At the same time, a huge amount of work and reporting went into the memorial concert at the Staples Center. The request for tickets from all over the world was overwhelming. Jermaine Jackson revealed that "there are twenties of thousands just from the UK. We worked with the (Los Angeles) city authorities and they are trying their best with the time-frame we have and we are hoping everybody is safe."

It was reported that the Staples Center is owned by AEG Live, the company organising the London gigs and it was there that rehearsals for the shows took place. AEG taped some of these rehearsals and the company released a small amount of video footage to the media. AEG's spin on Jackson's stilted performance in the video was that he simply wasn't going flat out while rehearsing but when necessary could turn it on, just like before. It looked worse than that to me. The TMZ website stated that AEG had invested almost "$30 million dollars in advance costs related to the London performances". Again, according to TMZ, about half of this amount was insured. I find it hard to believe that any company, let alone one as experienced as AEG, would spend double on advance costs than they insured, particularly in Jackson's case since he was known to be somewhat frail. I would also have expected AEG to have insured themselves against any loss arising from Jackson's inability to perform at one or all of the concerts. The risk would be just too great. To date, Randy Phillips, the head of AEG, has been less than forthcoming over what arrangements were in place.

While all this was going on, something didn't seem right to me.

Of course thoughts persisted as to what caused the fatal heart attack. According to the respected celebrity biographer, Ian Halperin, it was the "gruelling preparation for the O2 concerts in London" that ultimately killed him. A documentary shown on British television seemed to be claiming that Jackson had given up prescription drugs in a bid to get fit for the London gigs and it was this sudden withdrawal that caused the cardiac arrest.

My memory turned to an incident that occurred in 2007 when Jackson was due to make a long-awaited comeback at the World Music Awards, held at Earls Court in London, where he was due to sing. Once again, the media descended into an absolute frenzy. There had been talk of new recordings but as time passed nothing more had been heard of them, so attention was focused on the upcoming performance. What happened that night was something so unlikely it is a wonder that anyone believed it. But believe it they did. It fed the Michael Jackson myth-machine so well that nobody thought to look further than the lurid tale that accompanied the performance. Or rather the non-performance as it turned out.

At the appointed moment, there was no sign of Jackson on the stage. After World Music Awards workers were dispatched to discover what was going on, the singer was eventually found by Beyonce Knowles lying in the foetal position in his dressing room, unable to perform because, as he told Beyonce, he had "stage fright". Now Michael Jackson had been performing almost from the day he was born. He may have suffered from many things in his life but stage fright was not one of them. When he eventually took to the stage he gave perhaps the most lacklustre performance of his career. To my admittedly untrained eye he looked totally stoned. Or worse! He displayed classic signs of poisoning. Was this a harbinger of things to come?

2.

The incident at Earls Court was merely a very public manifestation of a private deterioration in Jackson's condition that had been underway for many years. But the appearance in London showed a marked descent into something beyond the addiction to prescription drugs which had been so obvious at his trial. After his death I confided to a few close confidantes that I was not satisfied with the stated cause and believed that the singer might have been the victim of foul play. Most dismissed my concerns as preposterous.

Then on 8 July 2009 the website TMZ once more provided an exclusive story which would gather momentum in the coming days and weeks. Numerous law enforcement agencies, the website claimed, were beginning a murder enquiry into Michael Jackson's death. The investigators were looking at the actions of Jackson's personal physician, Dr Conrad Murray, who had been hired by AEG to look after the singer's medical needs at something approaching $100,000 a month. It was widely thought that Jackson was addicted to prescription drugs, particularly Valium and Lorezepam, but Murray publicly denied a rumour that he had injected the singer with one or more of these preparations. The Beverley Hills police also sought to to get hold of Jackson's medical records, to talk to Jackson's former dermatologist, Dr Arnold Klein, and to other doctors who had recently treated him. The LA police chief, William Bratton, asked the pertinent questions when cornered by journalists. "Are we dealing with a homicide? Or are we dealing with an accidental overdose?"

Following this revelation, all hell broke loose. Michael's father, Joe Jackson, told ABC News that he believed his son was the victim of "foul play". La Toya Jackson went even further, telling the British newspaper, *The News of the World*, "Michael was murdered. I know who did it and I won't rest until I nail them." Without naming names, she added some detail. "We don't think just one person was involved. Rather, it was a conspiracy of people. Michael was worth over a billion in music publishing assets and somebody killed him for that. He was worth more dead than alive."

As we have seen, the largest beneficiary of Jackson's music publishing interests was Sony. Was La Toya pointing the finger at the Japanese corporation as somehow being involved in his death? I would also reiterate that La Toya's estimate of Sony ATV's value was way short. The company is well on the way to being worth $5 billion. Its value has been consistently underestimated down the years. Meanwhile, Michael's brother, Tito, blamed Dr Conrad Murray for "dithering" while Michael died. "I don't know what the time lapse was between the doctor finding him and when he called paramedics," Tito explained, "but I believe if he had immediately called for help we might still have my brother here today; he would definitely still be alive." Jermaine Jackson also blamed Dr Murray, saying, "A doctor is supposed to keep someone alive. But Michael went from good health to death in the space of one day."

Then, on July 22, federal investigators raided Dr Murray's clinic in Houston, Texas. An anonymous police source told the media that they believed Dr Murray had "administered a powerful anaesthetic that killed him." It wasn't long before Murray's home and office in Las Vegas were similarly visited by agents with a search warrant.

Enter Propofol.

3.

Propofol is an anaesthetic used in surgery. It produces unconsciousness almost immediately. It is said that when you wake up from it you feel absolutely incredible. It is easy to see why some people might get addicted to it, so total are its effects.

Propofol, which is known in North America as Diprivan, first came onto the market in the 1980s. Because of its efficiency in putting people to sleep, it soon became the drug of choice for anaesthetists. I spoke about its properties to Professor Greg McLatchie, one of the world's greatest surgeons and author or editor of a number of textbooks published by The Oxford University Press and Harvard University. His *Surgeons' Handbook* is used throughout the world. Professor McLatchie described the drug. "It is an induction agent for anaesthesia" he said. "It is used in operations and has to be monitored continuously. In its first stage it can cause breathing to stop, although this is usually transient. It is administered in very small doses – a one percent solution – either intravenously or by infusion. It should always be accompanied by a resuscitation regime as it can raise potassium levels which can cause heart failure." When I asked him if he knew of any circumstances in which he might prescribe and administer Propofol to an individual in his own home for some kind of pain relief or other reason not connected with surgery, he replied immediately. "I would never use it in that manner and I would be surprised if any doctor answered otherwise."

It took only five years from its introduction for the first incidences of addiction to Propofol to be reported. At the time its use was confined to medical practitioners but it was not long before its properties became more widely known. Even so, its non-medical usage remains extremely rare, not least because it has to be injected or infused and addicts have to repeat the injection process up to one hundred times a day, due to the short action of the high. It often requires a local anaesthetic to be administered at the same time to reduce the painful nature of infusion. Normally, the local anaesthetic used is called Lidocaine. It is not clear how long Propofol remains in the system or whether it shows up easily in toxicology tests. To my knowledge, Propofol has rarely, if ever, been looked at as a cause of death of an individual who died in his own home. It should be obvious from the above that, unless you are undergoing a surgical procedure, Propofol should be avoided at all costs. Unfortunately, research has tended to show that its oblivion-inducing properties have made it attractive to those who have suffered deep psychological trauma, particularly certain forms of childhood abuse. This is what may have drawn Michael Jackson to it.

However, as Professor McLatchie so adamantly maintained, no responsible doctor would countenance its prescription to anyone outside the operating room. A registered nurse, Cherilyn Lee, who had attended Jackson in the past, told Associated Press that she repeatedly "rejected his demands" that she give him Propofol. So the question arises: what on earth did Dr Conrad Murray think he was doing administering this most dangerous of drugs to the King of Pop?

Michael Jackson had many personal physicians over the years. What began as a necessary adjunct to his entourage following his burning accident while shooting the advertisement for Pepsi Cola, gradually morphed into providers of hard-core prescription drugs. Jackson was one of those unlucky people who, having been properly supplied with prescription-only pain-killers, became addicted to them and would feel extremely ill if he didn't have them. Like others who suffered a similar fate, the drugs supplied included Valium, Lorazepam and sometimes Ephedrine, a stimulant.

However, from even the strongest pain-killers – the opiates – the move to Propofol was exponential. It is not even a pain-killer, it is an extremely powerful anaesthetic. The statement of Professor McLatchie tells us that it should never be given in a manner that might occur with more conventional pain-relief preparations.

It is therefore important to look at the circumstances in which it was prescribed and administered, which parties colluded in it being made available to Jackson and what was to be gained by such collusion.

4.

Dr Conrad Murray graduated from the Meharry Medical College School of Medicine in the top fifty percent of his class in 1989. Meharry is not a top-notch medical school but perhaps one in the second rank of such institutions in the USA. His specialties are internal medicine, cardiology and cardiovascular disease. He landed a fellowship at the University of Arizona in 1995 and was appointed to the Foundation for Cardiovasular Medicine in San Diego the following year. Given the knowledge of the heart and its processes he must have obtained through specialising in these areas, it is even more incredible that he administered Propofol to Michael Jackson. In the USA, medics are not licensed nationally as they are in most countries. There, doctors acquire their licenses from a particular state where they carry out their practice. In Dr Murray's case, he was licensed to practice in Texas, Nevada and California.

Jackson was not known for having any heart problems. So what was a cardiologist doing becoming his personal physician? It is thought that the singer might have been referred to Dr Murray for some sort of tests to be carried out, probably for insurance purposes relating to the comeback gigs at the 02. It was beginning to become apparent that certain facts did not add up. Why did a cardiologist leave his supposedly lucrative practices to become a personal doctor, subject to the whims of a star? And why did he administer to that star one of the most noxious drugs possible? To answer this, we must look at Dr Murray's paymasters.

5.

Conrad Murray was engaged, not by Michael Jackson, but the company AEG Live, which was the organisation promoting the fifty comeback gigs at London's O2 – the *This Is It* tour. Contractually, it appears that the Jackson camp, which no longer included his ubiquitous spokesperson, Raymone Bain (she decided to sue Jackson for what she claimed was $29 million in unpaid fees), but did see a return to the fold once again of Jackson's long-time lawyer and manager, John Branca, ceded a number of key appointments to AEG Live, including the crucial position of personal physician. Exactly what his brief was remains unclear. And by how far that brief extended to providing the star with dangerous substances for non-medical reasons is a matter of speculation. It would seem likely, though, that the issue of Jackson's drug taking must have been addressed at some point if only to ensure compliance with any insurance terms. Michael Jackson did not have a history of not turning up for concerts: That only occurred on a very few occasions. He was, however, known to be in physical pain and mental turmoil. In that scenario, insurance would certainly be made available by Lloyds of London, although the presence of an approved doctor would be an essential condition of the policy. AEG Live, under the watchful eyes of its CEO, Randy Phillips, would have been tasked with overseeing all of this.

AEG Live is a wholly owned subsidiary of the Anschutz Entertainment Group, and is the second biggest concert and sports promoter in the world, after Live Nation. In recent times it has promoted tours by the likes of Justin Timberlake, Christina Aguilera, Bon Jovi, Usher and Prince, as well as various festivals across the USA. AEG also owns a number of lucrative sports franchises, including the LA Galaxy soccer team. It was the company that underwrote the huge amount of money – in excess of $100 million – it took to lure David Beckham from Real Madrid to Southern California.

AEG, however, is itself a wholly-owned subsidiary of the Anschutz Corporation, a US holding company formed in 1958 which now has interests in at least one hundred businesses. It is the private fiefdom of one man, the billionaire, Philip Anschutz.

Anschutz hails from the west, where his father was a land speculator who moved into oil. When Anshcutz inherited the old man's business, he turned it into a giant, and upon the sale of fifty percent of the oil interests to Mobil for $500 million in 1982 Anschutz embarked on an ambitious expansion policy, taking in newspapers, movie theatres, railroads and telecommunications. All of this propelled him to become the thirty-first richest man in America, with an estimated fortune in 2008 of $7.8 billion. While his career seemed to go from success to success, he was accused of inflating the profits of one of the companies he founded – Qwest – then selling his own shares at a massive profit. Anschutz settled the case with some huge charitable donations. In 1999, Fortune magazine called him the country's "greediest executive".

There is another, altogether more sinister side to Anschutz's operations, however. It is a hidden agenda much like that of the Sony Corporation. Sony, remember, was always first and foremost a commercial enterprise but behind it lay the almost mystical ideas of its founders to be a repository for the honour of Japan. This was the fervour that had previously been invested in the Emperor. Similarly Philip Anschutz has motives that go beyond mere commercial success. What both companies have in common is that what they regard as the best-case scenario is the convergence of the twin objectives. This creates a 'perfect storm' where making money and the hidden agendas can be realised in the same activity.

In Philip Anschutz's case, his corporation is dedicated to furthering the ideology of America's Christian conservatives. Anschutz was a huge supporter of the neocon project that was the driving force behind the Bush-Cheney regime. Just because Bush is no longer in power, it does not mean that the people associated with the project have gone away. On the contrary, despite being roundly beaten in the presidential election, they are turning their attentions to new strategies.

To those outside the USA, it is difficult to understand how important the recent 'culture wars' have been to the country. They have pitted social conservatives, including and often led by, the protestant evangelical movement, against the more traditional liberal-conservative values that held sway in the USA from the Democratic presidency of Franklin Roosevelt onward. This evangelical movement, which is often at odds with more traditional forms of the religion, has had great influence on the modern Republican Party, at least since the era of Ronald Reagan. Philip

Anschutz is a leading member of this constituency. He has been in the forefront of campaigns against abortion and gay rights and has overseen a massive amount of political lobbying for his cause. Moreover, he created the Discovery Foundation which promotes the concept of 'intelligent design' (a euphemism for what was previously called creationism) and vigorously opposes Darwin's theory of evolution. The Discovery Foundation is in the vanguard of the movement to rid America of Darwinian science and replace it with a literal interpretation of the Book of Genesis. It is the sacred duty of such zealots to cleanse the world of what they regard as sin and error. Anschutz has deployed both his money and his influence in his quest to further these conservative Christian values.

The reader may be forgiven for thinking, at this point, that Philip Anschutz's religious beliefs are of minor importance in the operation of his business activities. But to Christian fundamentalists nothing is more important than their religious convictions. And at the extreme edge of this belief-system is faith in the End of Days and belief in the Rapture and prophecies contained in the Book of the Revelation. I can speak with some authority on these matters. I am an Associate of Kings College, which means I have studied these ideas to a high level under some of the world's most eminent theologians. I can say with certainty that those who are true believers will stop at nothing to ensure the day comes to pass when the prophecies are realised.

As far as Anschutz is concerned, if anyone doubts his commitment to the cause, consider the following comment, made by an anonymous colleague of his to Fortune magazine. "He (Anschutz) has a latent interest in doing something significant in American Christianity. He is working deliberately and diligently on it."

On examination, it seems that the whole thrust of Anschutz's activities in recent years has been concerned, as he sees it, to bring America back to God. Not in the meek and mild sense we associate with the Christian message these days but with a warlike and belligerent attitude that condemns unbelievers to the fires of hell.

It was these forces which drove Anschutz to move into the entertainment industry. As the writer Justin Clark said in 2006, Anschutz is determined to "bring conservative Christianity to Hollywood".

Anschutz's ventures in the movie business seem to confirm this. His company made *The Chronicles of Narnia* and *The Lion, The Witch and The*

Wardrobe, both of which are allegories of the Christian story. He is also said to have personally intervened in the editing of the film *Ray,* the biopic of Ray Charles, to take out many of the references to Charles's drug taking and womanising and to play up the more Christian aspects of Charles's life such as his gospel connections.

So what are we to make of Anschutz's dealings with Michael Jackson? After all, Jackson was a tainted brand, particularly in America after his trial. In all probability it started out as an exercise to promote the profile and profitability of one of Anschutz's flagship operations, the O2 arena in London and steal a march on the world's number one promoter, Live Nation. But it was not long before other issues surfaced that, to Anschutz, were more compelling.

6.

It is often said in the media that the 02 is 'owned' by AEG Live. In fact it is owned by the British Government, having been built as part of the turn-of-the-century celebrations and named The Millennium Dome. Constructed at a cost of $1.3 billion it soon became a white elephant and an embarrassment to the Government. Although it was originally meant to be a temporary structure, its very public failure ensured that the Government would look around for an alternative use. It was subsequently leased for 999 years to a consortium of two property companies, Quintain and Lend Lease. They in turn granted management rights to AEG Live. At the time of writing, discussions are taking place between Quintain and Trinity College, of the University of Cambridge, to buy the 999 year lease.

It thus fell to AEG Live's CEO, Randy Phillips, to turn it into a profitable venue. By the time Michael Jackson was recruited, AEG Live was certainly beginning to make a success of the rebranded 02. High profile sports events and concerts were giving it the reputation of one of the leading venues in the world. It would just take one more coup to seal its growing status and allow AEG to really challenge Live Nation. It was in this atmosphere that Randy Phillips turned to Michael Jackson.

The mere mention of Jackson set off waves of media coverage for both the 02 and AEG Live. The man at the top, Philip Anschutz, stayed in the background but as we have seen, he was more than likely to be involved when necessary. At first, AEG told Jackson they wanted him to do ten concerts. That would have been a manageable number and would not cost too much if anything went wrong, as easily it might given Jackson's recent state of mind and body.

The ten shows sold out within minutes. As Jackson had not given a proper live performance in years, no-one could have known the massive impact his comeback would have. It was at this pivotal moment that the decision was taken to extend the number of shows to fifty. There is some dispute as to whether Jackson was made aware of the increase. What is beyond dispute is that AEG Live had lost their heads in the incredible amount of publicity and ticket sales that ensued when Jackson announced these would be his last shows. Randy Phillips and his backers were carried away on a tide of Michael Jackson hype which was normal for the singer but a new experience for them, even though they had hosted huge artists at the 02, like Prince.

At first it did not look bad. On the contrary, everything was going from strength to strength. The fifty concerts sold out in an hour. Seven hundred and fifty thousand tickets were snapped up by people from all over the world. It looked like the coup AEG was looking for.

It did not take long, however, for Randy Phillips to become deeply concerned and it was his duty to pass on those concerns to his bosses at the parent company. Jackson's mental and physical condition was not good. If anything he was deteriorating. So along with the legions of dancers, musicians, sound and lighting operatives, choreographers and the small army of technicians required to stage full rehearsals, Dr Conrad Murray was added to the list. His job was twofold. To monitor Jackson's health and report to AEG, while at the same time administering whatever was necessary by way of drugs to keep the show on the road. Soon, the first few shows were postponed because of Jackson's health, and this was followed by a downturn in rehearsal hours. Now things did not look good at all. The rehearsals that did take place saw Jackson unable to make the complicated dance steps that were his trademark or to summon up the full potential of his magnificent voice.

It was time for a review of the options.

7.

According to Ian Halperin, whose reports can generally be trusted as accurate, on the last night of Jackson's life, the star was "over the edge". He was "crying for his father, Joe", then began "reading the bible over and over again". Somewhat more sinisterly, Halperin claims that Jackson accused those charged with organising his comeback, none other than AEG, of "betrayal". He then called for Dr Murray to "put him out". This sounds like a full-blown psychotic episode to me, although Jackson now seemed to be harbouring genuine misgivings about AEG. The last thing a doctor should do in this situation is administer Propofol.

Did Dr Murray refer Jackson's behaviour to his employers when he was called to give the star the 'oblivion drug' or ask for any guidance? If so, what would that guidance have been? Furthermore, was Dr Murray able to discern whether the singer's behaviour was a precursor to cancelling the concerts? If this is so, what would that have meant for AEG and Philip Anschutz? It's time to look at some kind of audit of AEG's association with the King of Pop.

The ticket sales brought in over $100 million, with much more to follow from merchandising, recordings of the concerts and the video footage. A successful series of concerts would also invigorate Jackson's recording career generally and should have led to a new record which could have sold tens of millions. However, if Jackson failed to appear at all, this income would be lost as most people would want their ticket money back, no merchandise would be sold and any thoughts of a revival in Jackson's career would be over. Insurance payments would cover some of this but the huge outlay that AEG Live had already spent, estimated at anything up to $30 million, would be lost. This would not be good for AEG, desperate to catch up with the world's leading promoter, Live Nation. Its aspirations would be dashed right there and that in turn would reflect badly on Philip Anschutz and his Christian pretensions.

Perhaps the decision was taken at that point to look for a Plan B. If Jackson really was in terrible health then maybe that would minimise the losses and the bad publicity. Knowing Anschutz's anti-drug message, was it then that Dr Conrad Murray began to play fast and loose with the medications he was prescribing for and administering to, Michael Jackson? It was around this time that Jackson's demeanour began to go rapidly downhill and he appeared stoned or poisoned. It was only a short step from there to becoming embroiled in the mad world that had been created around Jackson and for the fatal overdose to be given.

The next question arising from all this is: who else, apart from Sony, has benefited from the death of Michael Jackson? The most obvious beneficiary is actually AEG. With Jackson deceased, his 'brand' was transformed overnight. Suddenly, most of those who had bought tickets wanted to keep them as souvenirs and did not ask for their money back. And AEG put before the court which was deciding on issues to do with Jackson's estate, a massive merchandising plan. It involved the usual teddy bears, mugs and wallpaper, which were all there to create a more sanitised version of Jackson: more 'cuddly', more 'Christian', and stripped of all the adverse factors that had been around for so long. Just as Philip Anschutz approached the movie of the dead Ray Charles's life, so would Jackson's merchandising follow the same template. In addition to the usual merchandise was a whole new raft of proposals for cashing in on the star's death, including ringtones, iPhone applications, screensavers and avatars for Second Life usage. Branding expert, Andy Milligan, put it best when he told the BBC, "When a brand survives a downturn, then makes a comeback, as has happened to Michael Jackson since his death, it comes back even stronger than before. Having seen off the negatives, there is not much more you can throw at it."

The other major beneficiary is, of course, our old friend, Sony. It is inconceivable to me that there would have been no contact between AEG and the Japanese when Jackson was hired for the 02 concerts. Sony, after all, owned all of Jackson's main recordings. However, that paled into insignificance compared to the hit Sony would take if the shows were so good that they revived Jackson's career – with another record company. That though, is an educated extrapolation. Could I actually find any solid connection between Sony and AEG? The answer to that question is an emphatic 'yes'.

After Jackson's death another request was made to the probate court. This time it was to ask the judge to approve a massive deal between AEG and Sony. With unseemly haste, while the Jackson family were dealing with the court over child-care arrangements and without having negotiated with any of the other major players, AEG agreed to sell to Sony's movie operation, Columbia, which had been acquired from the old CBS in 1990, all the film footage from Jackson's rehearsals. The number of hours of film contained in this deal was put at anything from 100 to 1200. It was to be edited down to produce a movie lasting about 150 minutes, directed by Kenny Ortega, who was responsible for *High School Musical*. Columbia was to pay AEG $60 million for the privilege. So Sony now had not only a monopoly on the sales of Jackson's recordings, but also a sure fire movie hit that could not have been made if the singer had still been alive. All courtesy of Philip Anschutz and his corporation, who would keep enough control to ensure the 'Christianisation' of the Jackson image.

It is true that in both the merchandising and film deals, AEG agreed to pay the lion's share of any profits to the Jackson estate, keeping a mere ten percent for itself. However, profits only start to accrue once all costs have been met. These costs could stretch into infinity, as they did when Sony spent so much to such little effect when they marketed '*Invincible*'.

The last question is this: why would Sony rush to help Philip Anschutz get out of the hole created by the Jackson deals? Hadn't the Japanese been desperate to offload Jackson after his acquittal in 2006? The answer to that lies in events that occurred in 2007, when Sony was about to release the film *The Da Vinci Code*.

The problem for Sony was that a huge amount of money, time and kudos had been invested in acquiring and producing *The Da Vinci Code*. But because the original book – which is one of the world's all-time best-sellers – relentlessly questioned established Christian theology, a backlash had developed among Christians, especially in the United States, who were lobbying to boycott the film. If the boycott had been successful, that would have been a disaster for Sony, which had much riding on the venture. They had every reason to believe they might be faced with such a problem. The response to the Mel Gibson film, *The Passion of the Christ*, was such that it showed the Christian lobby in full flow and what it could achieve. It was a group which, Sony thought, could make or break *The Da Vinci Code*. And such were Sony's worldwide losses since the massive investment in the new Playstation and the associated Blu-Ray system of high definition video, the company could not afford for *The Da Vinci Code* to fail.

So Sony decided on an unusual course of action. They mounted a charm offensive within the evangelical community. One of those they turned to was Philip Anschutz, who, as we have seen, has been a leading light in the movement for many years. Anschutz smoothed the path for Sony and *The Da Vinci Code*, possibly because its beef was more with the Roman

Catholic Church against which Protestants have been at war for centuries. In return, when it came to the crunch, Sony was ready to return the favour and resume its alliance with Anschutz, even to the extent of becoming involved once again with Michael Jackson, albeit a now dead and sainted Jackson.

Thus was Michael Jackson worth more dead than alive.

On 28 August 2009, the Los Angeles county coroner's report into Michael Jackson's death was made public. The star died from "acute Propofol intoxication". Also present were the drugs Valium and Lorazepam, along with the stimulant Ephedrine. The report meant that Jackson's death was now officially a homicide.

It is important to make clear that I am not accusing Dr Murray, Philip Anschutz or Sony with the murder of Michael Jackson, even if his death does have the ring of at least manslaughter about it. What I am saying is that I believe I have put forward enough evidence here to warrant a full-scale investigation of all those involved in the singer's last days. It is vitally important that any investigation should not confine itself to the hapless doctors who, after all, were employed by others named in this book. The US authorities can call for documents, subpoena records and interview those concerned to ascertain how far up the food-chain responsibility lies. I urge the authorities to act on this information. Only then will we be able finally to deliver justice to Michael Jackson and his family.

MICHAEL JACKSON SOLO DISCOGRAPHY

Got To Be There
Released: 1972   Label: Motown

Songs:

Ain't No Sunshine
Girl Don't Take Your Love From Me
Got To Be There
In Our Small Way
I Wanna Be Where You Are
Love Is Here And You Are Gone
Maria (you were the only one)
Rockin' Robin
Wings Of My Love
You've Got a Friend

Ben
Released: 1972   Label: Motown

Songs:

Ben
Everybody's Somebody's Fool
Greatest Show On Earth
In Our Small Way
My Girl
People Make The World Go Round
Shoo-be-Doo-be-Doo-da-Day
We've Got a Good Thing Going

What Goes Around Comes Around
You Can Cry On My Shoulder

Off The Wall
Released: 1979   Label: Epic

Songs:

Don't Stop 'till You Get Enough
Rock With You
Working Day and Night
Get On The Floor
Off The Wall
Girlfriend
She's Out Of My Life
Burn This Disco Out
It's The Falling In Love
I Can't Help It

Thriller
Released: 1982   Label: Epic

Songs:

Wanna Be Startin' Somethin'
Baby Be Mine
The Girl Is Mine
Thriller
Beat It
Billy Jean
Human Nature
P.Y.T.
The Lady In My Life

Farewell My Summer Love
Released: 1984   Label: Motown

This is a poor cash-in compilation

Bad
Released: 1987   Label: Epic

Songs:

Bad
The Way You Make Me Feel
Speed Demon
Liberian Girl
Just Good Friends
Another Part Of Me
Man In The Mirror
I Just Can't Stop Loving You
Dirty Diana
Smooth Criminal
Leave Me Alone

Dangerous
Released: 1991   Label: Epic

Songs:

Jam
Why You Wanna Trip On Me
In The Closet
She Drives Me Wild
Remember The Time
Can't Let Her Get Away
Heal The World

Black Or White
Who Is It
Give In To Me
Will You Be There
Keep The Faith
Gone Too Soon
Dangerous

HIStory: Past, Present and Future, Book One
(two disc set)
Released: 1995   Label: Epic

Songs:

Scream
They Don't Care About Us
Stranger In Moscow
This Time Around
Earth Song
D. S.
Money
Come Together
You Are Not Alone
Childhood
Tabloid Junkie
2 Bad
HIStory
Little Susie
Smile
Billie Jean
The Way You Make Me Feel
Black Or White
Rock With You

She's Out Of My Life
Bad
I Just Can't Stop Loving You
Man In The Mirror
Thriller
Beat It
The Girl Is Mine
Remember The Time
Don't Stop Till You Get Enough
Wanna Be Startin' Somethin'
Heal The World

Blood On The Dance Floor: HIStory In The Mix
Released 1997   Label: Epic

Songs:

Blood On The Dance Floor
Morphine
Superfly Sister
Ghosts
It Is Scary
Blood:
Scream Louder (Flyte Tyme)
Money (Fire Island Radio Edit)
2 Bad (Refugee Camp Mix)
Stranger In Moscow (Tee's In House Club Mix)
This Time Around (D. M. Radio Mix)
Earth Song (Club Experience)
You Are Not Alone (Classic Club Mix)
HIStory (Tony Moran's History Lesson)

The Best of Michael Jackson
(two disc set)
Released, 1998   Label, Motown

This was a low-budget, and, quite frankly, appalling attempt by Motown to cash in on Jackson's success during the nineties.

Ripples And Waves
Released, 2000   Label, Motown-Universal

Yet another dreadful compilation.

Invincible
Released 2001   Label: Epic

Songs:

Unbreakable
Heartbreaker
Invincible
Break of Dawn
Heaven Can Wait
You Rock My World
Butterflies
Speachless
2000 Watts
You Are My Life
Don't Walk Away
Privacy
Cry
The Lost Children
Whatever Happens

Number Ones
Released 2003   Label, Epic

Songs:

Don't Stop Till You Get Enough
Rock With You
Billie Jean
Beat It
Thriller
I Just Can't Stop Loving You
Bad
Smooth Criminal
The Way You Make Me Feel
Man In The Mirror
Dirty Diana
Black Or White
You Are Not Alone
Earthsong
You Rock My World
Break Of Dawn
One More Chance
Ben

WATCH THIS SPACE

INDEX

Index